By Lamplight

By Lamplight

Prose and verse chosen by
Elizabeth Hamilton and Charles Robertson

DUNEDIN PRESS
2002

First published by
DUNEDIN ACADEMIC PRESS LTD
Hudson House, 8 Albany Street, Edinburgh EH1 3QB, Scotland

ISBN 1 903765 06 4 (Cloth)
ISBN 1 903765 29 3 (Paperback)

Design by Mark Blackadder

Printed and bound by CPI Group

To Catherine

The Catherine to whom
this book is dedicated was the wife of the late
Major-General Sir John Kennedy, GCMG, KCMG, KCVO, KBF, CB, MC
Governor and Commander-in-Chief
Southern Rhodesia 1946–54.

She never knew what far-reaching consequences
her introduction to Yehudi was to have.

She died shortly after she had brought us together.

M ost simple things so beautifully are said,
They strike a glory in the quiet word,
As when the stillness of a twilight wood
Is broken by the singing of a bird.

Ann Lyon, 1907

Tribute to
Lord Menuhin OM KBE

PATRON, THE LAMP OF LOTHIAN
COLLEGIATE TRUST

With the recent sad death of Lord Menuhin the whole world was bereft, and our Haddington neighbourhood suffered an irreparable loss.

It is 30 years since he came at three weeks' notice, on fire with enthusiasm, to rescue a recently abandoned project to restore St Mary's Kirk, Haddington and to renew the cultural and artistic life of a 'whole' community. He succeeded. It was only a beginning. From then on he persuaded people to come and help us: a choreographer and a composer from New York came to produce an Auden play with East Lothian school children; pupils from his school, mostly from faraway places, came to take part in a variety of musical events. It was enormously stimulating and exciting and we could not have done what we did without him.

To begin with, he frequently came himself. With his help and encouragement the hitherto abandoned project grew and expanded.

Extraordinary things have happened. Music of a quality, to which many thought it was folly to aspire, is now regularly heard in and around St Mary's Kirk.

The Old Kirk Mill has become a centre for cultural and creative renewal beyond our wildest dreams and is now to receive a Lottery Grant.

None of this blossoming of creativity and of music and the Arts could have happened without Yehudi and the inspiration and quiet compulsion that he brought to bear.

He came seven times. The last time was in May 1997. Yehudi lit candles in dark places. The candles he lit will not go out for they are a witness to his joy in our achievement. Now they are our tribute to him.

HONORARY PRESIDENT
November, 2001

Foreword

In the nature of things, an anthology must contain material
which appeals to a wide variety of readers, to some more than to
others and perhaps to some not at all. This anthology comes from
lowland Scotland: some of the lyrics of Dunbar and Burns, for
example, may be almost incomprehensible to those who are
unfamiliar with the Lowland Scots speech, but they are not
inaccessible. I remember listening to the late Dr Jamie Richardson
of the Historic Buildings Council for Scotland reciting, on
request and without a moment's notice, Dunbar's *To a Ladye* and
how magical he made it.

As I collected my bundle of poems, the whole idea of *By
Lamplight* appealed to me more and more. Some of the 'greats'
could not be omitted: Scotland is part of the world to which
they belong.

The next move was a great step forward. I took my
growing bundle of poems to my friend The Reverend Charles
Robertson. His immediate response and his delight in the whole
project were inspirational. He was willing, moreover, not only to
make his own collection of verse and prose but to perform the
additional editorial tasks that a book would require.

Listening to poetry is like listening to music. It creates a
thirst for the beauty of it, and a sense of delight in its
enjoyment. This delight is my contribution to *By Lamplight*. I
offer it with special thanks to all those who have contributed to
the production of this book.

ELIZABETH HAMILTON

History

The Lamp of Lothian Trust (*The Lamp*) was set up in 1967. It
drew inspiration from the distant past which goes back directly to
the Christian renewal inspired by St Francis of Assisi and which
spread like wildfire through thirteenth century Europe. In its
wake a group of Franciscan brothers made their way to
Haddington in East Lothian. There they established a friary on
the banks of the Scottish Tyne where Holy Trinity Church now
stands. We are told that it was a church of wonderful beauty, the
choir from its elegance and clearness of light becoming known
as 'the Lamp of the Lothians'. Then in 1356, at Candlemas, the
church and friary were sacked by invading English armies.

Within 25 years, on a site a hundred yards upriver, a
church dedicated to St Mary was built. This new Lamp of the
Lothians shone briefly. In the campaign known as 'The Rough
Wooing' in 1548, when King Henry VIII of England sought the
hand of the infant Queen of Scots for his son, the future Edward
VI of England, Haddington was besieged and the choir of St
Mary's ruined and left open to the skies. A barrier wall was
erected between the nave and the ruin. It would be more than
400 years before the building was restored and used as a whole
church once more.

The name, *Lamp of the Lothians*, stood for a centre of
spiritual enlightenment. The people who gathered in medieval
churches looked and listened, their souls restored by noble archi-
tecture, singing choirs, and the glowing colours of paintings and
murals. As they received the consolations of word and sacrament,
every faculty of the aesthetic sense was brought into play. Recalling
this, we become aware of a unity long lost but still a compelling
source of inspiration. Moved by it, we embarked on a quest to
restore a 'whole church', to a whole or 'healed' community.

There has, as a consequence, been a burgeoning of life
and activity.

The 'Old Kirk Mill', down the road from St Mary's, now
houses studios, galleries, and workshops used by every age group
in the community.

A verse from *The Gude and Godlie Ballatis* (1567) enshrines and expresses our hope that others may benefit from our experience, and that elsewhere lamps may be lit to shed warmth and light on communities other than our own:

> *Go, hart, unto the lamp of licht.*
> *Go, hart, do service and honour,*
> *Go, hart, and serve Him day and nicht:*
> *Go, hart, unto thy Saviour.*

E.H.

Introduction

By Lamplight is arranged in sixteen sections of varying length. Each of the sections is introduced by a quotation, which announces the 'theme' for that section. The passages which follow illuminate the theme.

Each passage has been given a heading, occasionally the original title but more commonly a tag, to arrest the eye, arouse the imagination, and assist reflection on such basic and vital concepts as Light, Wisdom, Worship, Peace.

Spelling and punctuation have largely been left in their original forms, although occasionally they have been modernised in order to make the extracts as accessible as possible.

The *Notes on Sources and Authors* (pp. 254–285) are intended to add to the interest of the book.

C.R.

Contents

T he Inward Light is the light of Christ.
It is a universal Light,
which can be known by anyone,
of either sex, of whatever religion.

I

George Fox, 1624–1691

New Lamps Lit

Let Love's unconquerable might
Your scattered companies unite
In service to the Lord of light:

So shall God's will on earth be done,
New lamps be lit, new tasks begun,
And the whole world at last be one.

George Kennedy Allen Bell, 1883–1958

Love the Light

4

There is a light which made the light of the sun.
Let us love this light,
let us long to understand it,
let us thirst for it,
that with it as our guide
we may at length come to it
and so live in it that we may never die.

St Augustine, 354–430

Let Light Rule

O Light that never fades,
as the light of day now streams through these windows
and floods this room,
so let me open to thee the windows of my heart,
that all my life may be filled by the radiance of thy presence.
Let no corner of my being
be unillumined by the light of thy countenance.
Let there be nothing within me to darken the brightness
of the day.
Let the Spirit of him whose life was the light of men
rule within my heart till eventide.

John Baillie, 1886–1960

Three Dazzling Torches

Grant, O Lord, that I may give Thee choice gifts,
three lighted and dazzling torches:
My spirit, my soul, and my body,
my spirit to the Father,
my soul to the Son,
my body to the Holy Ghost.
> O Father, sanctify my spirit!
> O Son, sanctify my soul!
> O Holy Ghost, sanctify my sin-soiled body!

Eastern Church

The Kindling

Come, my Light, and illumine my darkness.
Come, my Life, and revive me from death.
Come, my Physician, and heal my wounds.
Come, Flame of divine love, and burn up the thorns of my sins,
    Kindling my heart with the flame of thy love.
Come, my King, sit upon the throne of my heart and reign there.
For thou alone art my King and my Lord.

St Dimitrii of Rostov, 17th century

The Lamplighter

My tea is nearly ready and the sun has left the sky;
It's time to take the window to see Leerie going by;
For every night at teatime and before you take your seat,
With lantern and with ladder he comes posting up the street.

Now Tom would be a driver and Maria go to sea,
And my papa's a banker and as rich as he can be;
But I, when I am stronger and can choose what I'm to do,
O Leerie, I'll go round at night and light the lamps with you!

For we are very lucky with a lamp before the door,
And Leerie stops to light it as he lights so many more;
And O! before you hurry by with ladder and with light,
O Leerie, see a little child and nod to him tonight!

Robert Louis Stevenson, 1850–1894

The Night Wanes

As from some Alpine watch-tower's portal
    Night, living yet, looks forth for dawn,
    So from time's mistier mountain lawn
The spirit of man, in trust immortal,
    Yearns toward a hope withdrawn.

The morning comes not, yet the night
    Wanes, and men's eyes win strength to see
    Where twilight is, where light shall be
When conquered wrong and conquering right
    Acclaim a world set free.

Algernon Charles Swinburne, 1837–1909

The Child of Light

If the scriptures had said: 'Today, light is born,'
man's heart would not have leapt.
The idea would not have become a legend
and would not have conquered the world.
They would merely have described a normal physical phenomenon
and would not have fired our imagination –
I mean our soul.
But the light which is born in the dead of winter
has become a child
and the child has become God,
and for twenty centuries our soul has suckled it . . .

Nikos Kazantzakis

Light of the World

II

Light of the world! for ever, ever shining,
    There is no change in Thee;
True Light of Life, all joy and health enshrining
    Thou canst not fade nor flee.

Thou hast arisen, but Thou descendest never;
    To-day shines as the past;
All that Thou wast Thou art, and shalt be ever,
    Brightness from first to last.

Night visits not Thy sky, nor storm, nor sadness;
    Day fills up all its blue, –
Unfailing beauty, and unfaltering gladness,
    And love for ever new.

Light of the world, undimming and unsetting!
    O shine each mist away;
Banish the fear, the falsehood, and the fretting;
    Be our unchanging Day.

Horatius Bonar, 1808–1889

With Thee there is Light

O God, early in the morning do I cry unto Thee.
Help me to pray, and to think only of Thee.
I cannot pray alone.
In me there is darkness,
but with Thee there is light.

I am lonely
but Thou leavest me not.
I am feeble in heart,
but thou leavest me not.
I am restless,
but with Thee there is peace.
In me there is bitterness,
but with Thee there is patience.
Thy ways are past understanding,
but Thou knowest the way for me.

Dietrich Bonhoeffer, 1906–1945

Light Fills our Life with Song

To you, O God, be glory and praise for ever!
You dwell in light unapproachable
but make visible the mystery of your presence.
In the changing year,
your light never fails.
You light the day with the sun's light,
and the midnight with shining stars.
You sent forth your Sun of Righteousness
to call us out of darkness into his marvellous light.
Through your kindness
healing dawns upon the world,
your grace gives joy to those who walk in shadow,
your light fills all our life with song.
To you, O God, be glory and praise for ever!

Common Order 1994

The Brambles Bright

All things doth long and countless time first draw from darkness,
then hide from light: and there is nothing that is beyond hope.

Lo, when we wade the tangled wood
In haste and hurry to be there,
Nought seems its leaves and blossoms good,
For all that they be fashioned fair.

But looking up, at last we see
The glimmer of the open light
From o'er the place where we would be:
Then grow the very brambles bright.

So now, amidst our day of strife,
With many a matter glad we play
When once we see the light of life
Gleam through the tangle of today.

William Morris, 1834–96

The Power of Twilight

Many are susceptible to the peculiar power of the twilight,
particularly in lonely places.
For me it can evoke figures I knew as a boy;
tranced hunting moments at the back of woods, in a glade,
eyes staring at a cleft rock,
ears hearkening for the inaudible.
Two orders of being, the visible and the invisible,
pause on the doorstep of this grey hour,
and which is going to advance upon you you hardly know.
Tension gets drawn out until it is time that is drawn out,
so thin, so fine, that its range becomes enormous.

Neil Miller Gunn, 1891–1973

A Dazzling Darkness

Through that pure Virgin-shrine –
That sacred veil drawn o'er thy glorious noon
That men might look and live as Glow-worms shine,
        And face the Moon:
    Wise Nicodemus saw such light
    As made him know his God by night.

Were all my loud, evil days
Calm and unhaunted as is thy dark Tent,
Whose peace but by some Angel's wing or voice
        Is seldom rent;
    Then I in Heaven all the year long
    Would keep, and never wander here.

But living where the Sun
Doth all things wake, and where all mix and tyre
Themselves and others, I consent and run
        To ev'ry myre,
    And by this world's ill-guiding light,
    Err more then I can do by night.

There is in God (some say)
A deep, but dazzling darkness; as men here
Say it is late and dusky, because they
        See not all clear;
    O for that night! where I in him
    Might live invisible and dim.

Henry Vaughan 1622–1695

Our Rainbow Arch

Lord of all being, throned afar,
Thy glory flames from sun and star;
Centre and soul of every sphere,
Yet to each loving heart how near!

Sun of our life, thy quickening ray
Sheds on our path the glow of day;
Star of our hope, thy softened light
Cheers the long watches of the night.

Our midnight is thy smile withdrawn,
Our noontide is thy gracious dawn,
Our rainbow arch thy mercy's sign;
All, save the clouds of sin, are thine.

Lord of all life, below, above,
Whose light is truth, whose warmth is love,
Before thy ever-blazing throne
We ask no lustre of our own.

Grant us thy truth to make us free
And kindling hearts that burn for thee,
Till all thy living altars claim
One holy light, one heavenly flame.

Oliver Wendell Holmes 1809–1894

Perfect Day in the Dead of Night

18 Abide with us, O most blessed and merciful Saviour,
for it is toward evening and the day is far spent.
As long as Thou art present with us, we are in the light.
When Thou art present, all is brightness, all is sweetness.
We discourse with Thee, live with Thee and lie down with Thee.
Abide then with us, O Thou whom our soul loveth;
thou Sun of righteousness with healing under Thy wings,
arise in our hearts.
Make Thy light then to shine in darkness,
as a perfect day in the dead of night.

Henry Vaughan 1622–1695

O God,
 help us not to despise or oppose
what we do not understand.

William Penn, 1644–1718

Adoration

Teach us to abide in the Light of thy Eternity,
    in simplicity, in stillness and in peace;
asking for nothing,
seeking to understand nothing,
but absorbed in that selfless adoration of thy Glory,
    which is the heart of prayer.

Evelyn Underhill (Mrs Stuart Moore), 1875–1941

The Wise Word

When men who have the same loyalty to our Lord sit together and discuss freely, frankly and courteously, they will find that for all practical needs they are given a common mind. In all assemblies of men of goodwill and common purpose, the important thing is to discern the Common Mind as it grows. For this purpose a man must come to the Council more desirous to learn than to teach, not thinking that he brings with him the sole and complete solution to any problem, but sure that what he brings will have its effect on the Common Mind and that a solution will be arrived at truer and completer than any member could have arrived at outside the Council.

Often the statement of extreme views on either side will have a balancing effect: bringing the Common Mind to an equilibrium; though the ultimate decision will reject the extravagance of both. The result will be, not a command or instruction, but a Wise Word, sent out to win its way by the wisdom and truth of its content. There is a natural impatience because it may take long to win its way and hence the desire to give the Council Executive and Administrative power, but there are few things greater than to be able to say the Wise and True Word. He that hath ears to hear, let him hear.

Bishop Palmer

Wingèd Words

Home, home from the horizon far and clear,
    Hither the soft wings sweep;
Flocks of the memories of the day draw near
    The dovecote doors of sleep.

Oh, which are they that come through sweetest light
    Of all these homing birds?
Which with the straightest and the swiftest flight?
    Your words to me, your words!

Alice Meynell, 1847–1922

A Noble Creed

Thou must be true thyself
If thou the truth wouldst teach
Thy soul must overflow, if thou
Another soul wouldst reach.
The overflow of heart it needs
To give the heart full speech.

Think truly, and thy thoughts
Shall the world's famine feed.
Speak truly and each word of thine
Shall be a truthful seed.
Live truly, and thy life shall be
A great and noble creed.

Source unknown

Invocation

Grant, O God, thy protection;
    And in protection, strength;
And in strength, understanding;
And in understanding, knowledge;
And in knowledge, knowledge of the truth;
And knowing the truth, to love it;
And when loving, to love all being;
And in all Being, to love God;
    God and all Goodness.

translated from Welsh by B G Evans

The Inward Sphere

26　The Hero is he who lives in the inward sphere of things, in the True, Divine and Eternal, which exists always unseen to most, under the Temporary, Trivial: his being is in that; he declares that abroad, by act or speech as it may be, in declaring himself abroad. His life . . . is a piece of the everlasting heart of Nature herself: all men's life is, – but the weak many know not the fact, and are untrue to it, in most times; the strong few are strong, heroic, perennial, because it cannot be hidden from them.

Thomas Carlyle, 1795–1881

The Shepherdess

She walks – the lady of my delight –
    A shepherdess of sheep.
Her flocks are thoughts. She keeps them white;
      She guards them from the steep;
She feeds them on the fragrant height,
    And folds them in for sleep.

She roams maternal hills and bright,
    Dark valleys safe and deep.
Into that tender breast at night
      The chastest stars may peep.
She walks – the lady of my delight –
    A shepherdess of sheep.

She holds her little thoughts in sight,
    Though gay they run and leap.
She is so circumspect and right;
      She has her soul to keep.
She walks – the lady of my delight –
    A shepherdess of sheep.

Alice Meynell, 1847–1922

Our God is a Consuming Fire

Fire melts wax and dries up mud: in the same way secret meditation melts our evil thoughts and withers the passions of the soul; it enlightens our mind, makes the understanding radiant, and drives away thoughts of wickedness. He who arms himself with this secret meditation, making his inner man resplendent, is strengthened by God, fortified by the angels, and glorified by men. Secret meditation and reading turns the soul into an impregnable stronghold, an invincible fortress, a peaceful haven, and they preserve it undisturbed and unshaken.

Secret meditation is a mirror for the mind and a light for the conscience; it tames lust, calms fury, dispels wrath, drives away bitterness, puts irritability to flight, and banishes injustice.

Secret meditation illuminates the mind and expels laziness. From it is born the tenderness that warms and melts the soul.

Secret meditation disperses evil thoughts, flogs the demons, sanctifies the body, teaches us long-suffering and restraint and keeps us mindful of Gehenna.

Secret meditation preserves the mind free of distractions and helps it to reflect upon death.

Secret meditation is full of every kind of good work, adorned with every virtue; and it is far removed from every evil deed.

St Isaias, 4th century AD

O God,
   make us children of quietness,
and heirs of peace.

St Clement AD 96

At Home

I asked for Peace –
My sins arose,
And bound me close,
I could not find release.

    I asked for Truth –
    My doubts came in,
    And with their din
    They wearied all my youth.

        I asked for Love –
        My lovers failed,
        And griefs assailed
        Around, beneath, above.

            I asked for Thee –
            And Thou didst come
            To take me home
            Within Thy heart to be.

D M Dolben, 1848–1877

The Ear of Faith

32

               I have seen
A curious child, who dwelt upon a tract
Of inland ground, applying to his ear
The convolutions of a smooth-lipped shell;
To which, in silence hushed, his very soul
Listened intensely; and his countenance soon
Brightened with joy; for from within were heard
Murmurings, whereby the monitor expressed
Mysterious union with its native sea.
Even such a shell the Universe itself
Is to the ear of Faith; and there are times,
I doubt not, when to you it doth impart
Authentic tidings of invisible things;
Of ebb and flow, and ever-during power;
And central peace, subsisting at the heart
Of endless agitation.

William Wordsworth, 1770–1850

Still Waters

As a white candle in a holy place,
So is the beauty of an aged face;
As the spent radiance of the winter sun,
So is a woman with her travail done,
Her brood gone from her, and her thoughts as still
As the waters under a ruined mill.

Joseph Campbell, 1879–1944

The Way of Peace

34 O Lord,
vouchsafe to look mercifully upon us,
and grant that we may ever choose the way of peace.

Sarum Missal, 15th century

Desire for Peace

Too late did I love you, O beauty of ancient days, yet ever new!
Too late did I love you.
And behold, you were within me and I was away from home,
and there I searched for you,
deformed, plunging,
absorbed in those beautiful forms which you had made.
You were with me, but I was not with you.
Things held me far from you,
things which would not have existed at all except for you.
You called, you shouted,
and burst in on my deafness.
You flared into light and gleamed brightly at me
and dispersed my blindness.
You breathed forth fragrances and I drew in breath,
and still I pant for you.
I tasted much, and still I hunger and thirst.
You touched me, and I burned with desire for your peace.

St Augustine, 354–430

The Given Peace

36

Show us, good Lord,
the peace we should seek,
     the peace we must give,
     the peace we can keep,
          the peace we must forgo,
          and the peace you have given
               in Jesus our Lord.

Contemporary Prayers for Public Worship, 1967

The White Peace

It lies not on the sunlit hill
    Nor on the sunlit plain:
Nor ever on any running stream
    Nor on the unclouded main –

But sometimes, through the Soul of Man,
    Slow moving o'er his pain,
The moonlight of a perfect peace
    Floods heart and brain.

William Sharp, 1855–1905

Still Dews of Quietness

38

Dear Lord and Father of mankind
    Forgive our foolish ways;
Reclothe us in our rightful mind;
In purer lives Thy service find,
    In deeper reverence, praise.

In simple trust like theirs who heard,
    Beside the Syrian sea,
The gracious calling of the Lord
Let us, like them, without a word
    Rise up and follow Thee.

O Sabbath rest by Galilee!
    O calm of hills above,
Where Jesus knelt to share with Thee
The silence of eternity,
    Interpreted by love!

With that deep hush subduing all
    Our words and works that drown
The tender whisper of Thy call,
As noiseless let Thy blessing fall
    As fell Thy manna down.

Drop Thy still dews of quietness,
    Till all our strivings cease;
Take from our souls the strain and stress,
And let our ordered lives confess
    The beauty of thy peace.

Breathe through the heats of our desire
    Thy coolness and Thy balm;
Let sense be dumb, let flesh retire;
Speak through the earthquake, wind, and fire,
    O still small voice of calm!

John Greenleaf Whittier, 1807–1892

Coronals of Roses

Peace, God's own peace,
This it is I bring you;
The quiet song of sleep,
Dear tired heart, I sing you.
Dream, softly dream,
Till solemn death shall find you,
With coronals of roses
Tenderly to bind you.
Peace past understanding,
Dear tired heart, I bring you;
The quiet song of evening
Softly I sing you.

Ivar Campbell, 1891–1916

Heaven-Haven

40

I have desired to go
    Where springs not fail,
To fields where flies no sharp and sided hail
    And a few lilies blow.

And I have asked to be
    Where no storms come,
Where the green swell is in the havens dumb,
    And out of the swing of the sea.

Gerard Manley Hopkins, 1844–1889

Endless Depth

To adore

That means to lose oneself; in the unfathomable,
to plunge into the inexhaustible,
to find peace in the incorruptible,
to be absorbed in defined immensity,
to offer oneself to the fire and the transparency,
to annihilate oneself
in proportion as one becomes more deliberately conscious of oneself,
and to give of one's deepest to that whose depth has no end.

Teilhard de Chardin 1881–1955

The Island Sanctuary

Here in the grass-grown chancel Prayer is a simple thing,
It mounts to the heart of God like a flight of birds
Seen through the great East window:
Linking earth and sky in a swift-rising arc
That soon escapes the frame of stone;
(For all its sculptured loveliness it cannot hold
Those upward-beating wings!)

The scent of thyme and heather
Blown from the hill, drifts through the unshut door:
Lingers and drifts like incense, till the very walls
Are steeped in fragrance.

Pray on;
Here is no man-made barrier to bar you from the altar
Where it stands, four-square,
Silvered with lichens, stained with rust-gold moss:
Washed by the rains of patient centuries.

Pray on;
And with what's left of the body's ear hear the chant of the sea . .
.

The wind's recitative . . . the wave's immense Amen . . .
And high above these, threading all sweet sound,
The curlew's descant mounting up . . . and up . . .
Until the silver circuit is complete,
And Prayer comes back transmuted into Power.

M H Noël Paton

Serving Peace

Lord, make me an instrument of your peace.;

> Where there is hatred, let me sow love,
> Where there is injury, pardon;
> Where there is doubt, faith;
> Where there is despair, hope;
> Where there is darkness, light;
> Where there is sadness, joy.

O divine Master, grant that I may not so much seek
To be consoled, as to console,
To be understood, as to understand,
To be loved, as to love,
For it is in giving that we receive;
It is in pardoning that we are pardoned;
It is in dying that we are born to eternal life.

St Francis of Assisi, 1181–1226

The Mighty Grasp

Twixt gleams of joy and clouds of doubt;
    Our feelings come and go;
Our best estate is tossed about
    In ceaseless ebb and flow.
No mood of feeling, form of thought,
    Is constant for a day;
But thou, O Lord, thou changest not:
    The same thou art alway.

I grasp thy strength, make it mine own,
    My heart with peace is blest;
I lose my hold, and then comes down
    Darkness, and cold unrest.
Let me no more my comfort draw
    From my frail hold of thee,
In this alone rejoice with awe –
    Thy mighty grasp of me.

Out of that weak, unquiet drift
    That comes but to depart,
To that pure heaven my spirit lift
    Where thou unchanging art.
Lay hold of me with thy strong grasp,
    Let thy almighty arm
In its embrace my weakness clasp,
    And I shall fear no harm.

Thy purpose of eternal good
    Let me but surely know;
On this I'll lean – let changing mood
    And feeling come or go –
Glad when thy sunshine fills my soul,
    Not lorn when clouds o'ercast,
Since thou within thy sure control
    Of love dost hold me fast.

John Campbell Shairp, 1819–1885

Worship is a transcendent wonder.

Thomas Carlyle, 1795–1881

The Secret

I met God in the morning;
    When my day was at its best,
And His presence came like sunrise,
    Like a glory in my breast.

All day long the Presence lingered,
    All day long He stayed with me,
And we sailed in perfect calmness
    O'er a very troubled sea.

Other ships were blown and battered,
    Other ships were sore distressed,
But the winds that seemed to drive them
    Brought to us a peace and rest.

But I thought of other mornings,
    With a keen remorse of mind,
When I too had loosed the moorings,
    With the Presence left behind.

So I think I know the secret,
    Learned from many a troubled way:
You must seek Him in the morning
    If you want Him through the day!

Ralph Spaulding Cushman

Just for Today

Lord,

> for tomorrow and its needs,
> I do not pray.
> Keep me, my God,
> From stain of sin
> Just for today.

>> Let me both
>> Diligently work
>> And duly pray.
>> And,
>> If today my tide of life should ebb away,
>> Give me, sweet Lord, thy Sacraments divine.

>>> So, for tomorrow and its needs
>>> I do not pray.
>>> But keep me, guide and love me, Lord,
>>> Just for today.

A Temple Meet

Between us and Thyself remove;
Whatever hindrances may be,
That so our inmost heart may prove
    A holy temple, meet for Thee.

Latin MSS, 15th Century

Before the Sacrament

Bread of the world in mercy broken,
    Wine of the soul in mercy shed!
By whom the words of life were spoken,
    And in whose death our sins are dead!

Look on the heart by sorrow broken,
    Look on the tears by sinners shed,
And be Thy feast to us the token
    That by Thy grace our souls are fed!

Reginald Heber, 1783–1826

Holy Communion

And now, O Father, mindful of the love;
That bought us once for all on Calvary's Tree,
And having with us him that pleads above,
    We here present, we here spread forth to thee
That only Offering perfect in thine eyes,
The one true, pure, immortal Sacrifice.

Look, Father, look on his anointed face,
    And only look on us as found in him;
Look not on our misusings of thy grace,
    Our prayer so languid and our faith so dim;
For lo, between our sins and their reward
We set the Passion of thy Son, our Lord.

And then for those, our dearest and our best,
    By this prevailing Presence we appeal;
O fold them closer to the mercy's breast;
    There shall they learn where lies their souls' true weal;
From tainting mischief keep them white and clear,
And crown thy gifts with grace to persevere.

And so we come: O draw us to thy feet,
    Most patient Saviour, who canst love us still;
And by this food, so awesome and so sweet,
    Deliver us from every touch of ill:
In thine own service make us glad and free,
And grant us nevermore to part from thee.

William Bright, 1824–1901

The Courts of the Lord

52 How lovely is thy dwelling place,
  O Lord of hosts, to me!
The tabernacles of thy grace
  how pleasant, Lord, they be!
My thirsty soul longs veh'mently,
  yea faints, thy courts to see:
My very heart and flesh cry out,
  O living God, for thee.

Behold, the sparrow findeth out
  an house wherein to rest;
The swallow also for herself
  hath purchased a nest;
Ev'n thine own altars, where she safe
  her young ones forth may bring,
O thou almighty Lord of hosts,
  who art my God and King.

Bless'd are they in thy house that dwell,
  they ever give thee praise.
Bless'd is the man whose strength thou art,
  in whose heart are thy ways.

Psalm 84: 1–5

God's Temple

O Holy Ghost, Comforter, Spirit of Truth,
     who art everywhere present and fillest all things,
        Treasure of Good, Giver of Life:
visit us, we beseech thee, with the fullness of thy grace.
Thou that hast sanctified these gifts (bread and wine),
sanctify us also, even our whole body, soul, and spirit,
that we may abide thy temple and dwelling place for ever.

The Liturgy of the Catholic Apostolic Church

The Beauty of Holiness

54

Honour and majesty are before the Lord:
      strength and beauty are in His sanctuary.
Give unto the Lord, O ye kindreds of the people,
      give unto the Lord glory and strength.
Give unto the Lord the glory due unto his name:
      bring an offering, and come into his courts.
O worship the Lord in the beauty of holiness:
      fear before Him, all the earth.

Psalm 96: 6–9

A Baby Sermon

The lightning and the thunder;
   They go and they come;
      But the stars and the stillness
        Are always at home.

George Macdonald, 1824–1905

A Blessing

May the love of the Lord Jesus;
    draw us to himself;
May the power of the Lord Jesus
    strengthen us in his service;
May the joy of the Lord Jesus
    fill our souls.

May the blessing of God almighty,
    the Father, the Son, and the Holy Ghost,
    be amongst you
    and remain with you,
        always.

William Temple, 1881–1944

I will make a covenant of peace: there shall be showers of blessing.

Ezekiel 34: 25, 26

St Columba's Blessing

May the wisdom of God guide you;
May the strength of God uphold you;
May the peace of God possess you;
May the love of God enfold you;
Now and to the end of days.

Source Unknown

Life is Good

Almighty God,
we lift up our hearts; in gratitude to Thee,
for all Thy loving-kindness.
We bless Thy Holy Name:
> for life and health,
> for love and friend-ship,
> and for Thy goodness and mercy
> that have followed us all the days of our life;
> for the wonder and beauty of the world,
> and for all things true and honest,
> just and pure,
> lovely and of good report.
We praise Thee, O God:
glory, thanks-giving, and praise be unto Thee.

Book of Common Order 1940

New Every Morning

Every day is a fresh beginning;,
    Listen my soul to the glad refrain.
    And, spite of old sorrows
       And older sinning,
       Troubles forecasted
       And possible pain,
Take heart with the day and begin again.

Susan Coolidge, 1835–1905

Think on These Things

Ask the loveliness of the earth,
ask the loveliness of the sea,
ask the loveliness of the wide airy spaces,
ask the loveliness of the sky;

ask the order of the stars,
ask the sun making the daylight with its beams,
ask the moon tempering the darkness of the night that follows;

ask the living things which move in the waters,
which tarry on the land,
which fly in the air;
ask the souls that are hidden,
the bodies that are perceptive,
the visible things which must be governed,
the invisible things which govern –

ask all these things, and they will answer you,
'Look, see, we are lovely.'
Their loveliness is their confession.
And these lovely but mutable things,
who has made them, save beauty immutable?

St Augustine, 354–430

Santa Teresa's Bookmark

Let nothing disturb thee,
Nothing affright thee;

All things are passing;
God never changeth;

Patient endurance
Attaineth to all things;

Who God possesseth
In nothing is wanting;
       Alone God sufficeth.

Henry Wadsworth Longfellow, 1807–1882

Blessings Make our Lives Delightful

64 Lord, we thank Thee for this place; in which we dwell;
for the love that unites us;
for the peace accorded us this day;
for the hope with which we expect the morrow;
for the health, the work, the food,
and the bright skies that make our lives delightful;
for our friends in all parts of the earth, and our friendly helpers.

Robert Louis Stevenson, 1850–1894

Our Daily Bread

Our Father, we thank Thee that –

> Back of the loaf is the snowy flour,
> And back of the flour is the mill,
> And back of the mill is the wheat and the shower,
> And the sun and the Father's will.

Anonymous

Live Safely, Sleep Softly

66 The Lord bless thee,
and keep thee:
the Lord make his face to shine upon thee,
and be gracious unto thee:
the Lord lift up his countenance upon thee,
and give thee peace.

Numbers 6: 24–27

I *find thee throned in my heart,*
my Lord Jesus.
It is enough.
I know that thou art throned in heaven.
My heart and heaven are one.

Gaelic, translated by Alistair MacLean, 1885–1936

His Blood upon the Rose

I see his blood upon the rose
And in the stars the glory of his eyes,
His body gleams amid eternal snows,
His tears fall from the skies.

I see his face in every flower;
The thunder and the singing of the birds
Are but his voice – and carven by his power
Rocks are his written words.

All pathways by his feet are worn,
His strong heart stirs the ever-beating sea,
His crown of thorns is twined with every thorn,
His cross is every tree.

Joseph Mary Plunkett, 1887–1916

That Holy Thing

They all were looking for a king
To slay their foes and lift them high;
Thou cam'st, a little baby thing
That made a woman cry.

O son of man, to right my lot
Nought but thy presence can avail;
Yet on the road thy wheels are not,
Nor on the sea thy sail!
Yea, every bygone prayer.

My fancied ways why should'st thou heed?
Thou com'st down thine own secret stair;
Com'st down to answer all my need,
Yea, every bygone prayer!

George Macdonald, 1824–1905

Angels of the Mist

If love should count you worthy, and should deign
 One day to seek your door and be your guest,
Pause! Ere you draw the bolt and bid him rest,
If in your old content you would remain,
For not alone he enters; in his train
Are angels of the mist, the lonely guest,
Dreams of the unfulfilled and unpossessed,
And sorrow, and Life's immemorial pain.

He wakes desires you never may forget,
He shows you stars you never saw before,
He makes you share with him, for evermore,
The burden of the world's divine regret.
How wise you were to open not! And yet,
How poor if you should turn him from the door!

Sidney Royse Lysaght, b. 1857

A Truer Beauty

O Christ, the Master Carpenter,
Who, at the last, through wood and nails,
purchased our whole salvation,
wield well your tools in the workshop of your world,
so that we, who come rough-hewn to your bench,
may here be fashioned to a truer beauty of your hand.

George F Macleod, 1895–1991

The Carpenter

Silent at Joseph's side he stood,
And smoothed and trimmed the shapeless wood,
And with firm hand, assured and slow,
Drove in each nail with measured blow.

Absorbed, he planned a wooden cask,
Nor asked for any greater task,
Content to make, with humble tools,
Tables and little children's stools.

Lord, give me careful hands to make
Such simple things as for thy sake,
Happy within thine house to dwell
If I make one table well.

Phyllis Hartnoll, b. 1906

The Mystery

He came and took me by the hand
    Up to a red rose tree,
He kept His meaning to Himself
    But gave a rose to me.

I did not pray Him to lay bare
    The mystery to me,
Enough the rose was Heaven to smell,
    And His own face to see.

Ralph Hodgson, 1871–1967

Our Lord and Our Lady

They warned Our Lady for the Child
That was Our blessed Lord,
And She took Him into the desert wild,
Over the camel's ford.

> And a long song She sang to Him
> And a short story told:
> And She wrapped Him in a woollen cloak
> To keep Him from the cold.

But when Our Lord was grown a man
The Rich they dragged Him down,
And they crucified Him in Golgotha,
Out and beyond the Town.

> They crucified Him on Calvary;
> Upon an April Day;
> And because He had been Her little Son
> She followed Him all the way.

Our Lady stood beside the Cross,
A little space apart,
And when She heard Our Lord cry out,
A sword went through Her heart.

> They laid Our Lord in a marble tomb,
> Dead, in a winding sheet.
> But Our Lady stands above the world
> With the white Moon at Her feet.

Hilaire Belloc, 1870–1953

Life in the Cross

O Love that wilt not let me go,
I rest my weary soul in thee:
I give thee back the life I owe,
That in thine ocean depths its flow
    May richer, fuller be.

O Light that followest all my way,
I yield my flickering torch to thee:
My heart restores its borrowed ray,
That in thy sunshine's blaze its day
    May brighter, fairer be.

O Joy that seekest me through pain,
I cannot close my heart to thee:
I trace the rainbow through the rain,
And feel the promise is not vain,
    That morn shall tearless be.

O Cross that liftest up my head,
I dare not ask to fly from thee:
I lay in dust life's glory dead,
And from the ground there blossoms red
    Life that shall endless be.

George Matheson, 1842–1906

The Cross Militant

May the Cross of the Son of God
who is mightier than all the hosts of Satan,
and more glorious than all the angels of heaven,
abide with you in your going out and your coming in!
By day and night, at morning and at evening,
at all times and in all places,
may it protect and defend you!
From the wrath of evil men,
from the assaults of evil spirits,
from foes invisible,
from the snares of the devil,
from all low passions that beguile the soul and body,
may it guard, protect, and deliver you.

The Christarakana

Let us Walk through the Door

Make no mistake: if He rose at all
it was as His body;
if the cell's dissolution did not reverse, the molecules
    reknit, the amino acids rekindle,
the Church will fall.

It was not as the flowers,
each soft Spring recurrent;
it was not as His Spirit in the mouths and fuddled
    eyes of the eleven apostles:
it was as His flesh: ours.

The same hinged thumbs and toes,
the same valved heart
that–pierced–died, withered, paused, and then
    regathered out of enduring Might
new strength to enclose.

Let us not mock God with metaphor,
analogy; sidestepping transcendence;
making of the event a parable, a sign painted in the
    faded credulity of earlier ages:
let us walk through the door.

The stone is rolled back, not papier-mâché,
not a stone in a story;
but the vast rock of materiality that in the slow
    grinding of time will eclipse for each of us
the wide light of day.
And if we will have an angel at the tomb,
make it a real angel,
weighty with Max Planck's quanta, vivid with hair,
    opaque in the dawn light, robed in real linen
spun on a definite loom.

Let us not seek to make it less monstrous,
for our own convenience, our own sense of beauty,
lest, awakened in one unthinkable hour, we are
        embarrassed by the miracle,
and crushed by remonstrance.

John Updike, b. 1933

To The Sun

O let your shining orb grow dim,
Of Christ the mirror and the shield,
That I may gaze through you to Him,
See half the miracle revealed,
And in your seven hues behold
The Blue Man walking on the sea;
The Green, beneath the summer tree,
Who called the children; then the Gold,
With palms; the Orange, flaring bold
With scourges; Purple in the garden
(As Greco saw); and then the Red
Torero (Him who took the toss
And rode the black horns of the cross –
But rose snow-silvered from the dead!)

Roy Campbell, 1901–1957

The Call

Come, my Way, my Truth, my Life:
Such a Way as gives us breath:
Such a Truth as ends all strife:
Such a Life as killeth death.

Come, my Light, my Feast, my Strength:
Such a Light, as shows a feast:
Such a Feast, as mends in length:
Such a Strength, as makes his guest.

Come, my Joy, my Love, my Heart:
Such a Joy, as none can move:
Such a Love, as none can part:
Such a Heart, as joys in love.

George Herbert, 1593–1633

The Shepherd Psalm

The Lord is my shepherd; I shall not want.
He maketh me to lie down in green pastures;
He leadeth me beside the still waters.
He restoreth my soul;
He leadeth me in the paths of righteousness for his name's sake.
Yea, though I walk through the valley of the shadow of death,
I will fear no evil: for thou art with me;
Thy rod and thy staff they comfort me.
Thou preparest a table before me in the presence of mine enemies.
Thou anointest my head with oil; my cup runneth over.
Surely goodness and mercy shall follow me all the days of my life.
And I will dwell in the house of the Lord for ever.

Psalm 23

Blessed art Thou, O Lord,
who hast revealed thyself in music,
and granted me the love of it.

Contemporary Hebrew

Words and Music

Bright is the ring of words;
    When the right man rings them,
Fair the fall of songs
    When the singer sings them.
Still they are carolled and said –
    On wings they are carried –
After the singer is dead
    And the maker is buried.

Low as the singer lies
    In the field of heather,
Songs of his fashion bring
    The swains together.
And when the west is red
    With the sunset embers,
The lover lingers and sings
    And the maid remembers.

Robert Louis Stevenson, 1850–1894

At a Solemn Music

Blest pair of Sirens, pledges of Heaven's joy,
Sphere-born harmonious sisters, Voice, and Verse!
Wed you divine sounds, and mixt power employ
Dead things with inbreathed sense able to pierce;
And to our high-raised phantasy present
That undisturbèd Song of pure concent
Ay sung before the sapphire-coloured throne
      To Him that sits thereon,
With saintly shout and solemn jubilee;
Where the bright Seraphim in burning row
Their loud uplifted angel-trumpets blow;
And the Cherubic host in thousand quires
Touch their immortal harps of golden wires,
With those just Spirits that wear victorious palms,
      Hymns devout and holy psalms
      Singing everlastingly:
That we on earth, with undiscording voice
May rightly answer that melodious noise;
As once we did, till disproportioned sin
Jarred against nature's chime, and with harsh din
Broke the fair music that all creatures made
To their great Lord, whose love their motion swayed
In perfect diapason, whilst they stood
In first obedience, and their state of good.
      O may we soon again renew that Song,
      And keep in tune with Heaven, till God ere long
      To his celestial consort us unite,
To live with him, and sing in endless morn of light!

John Milton, 1608–1674

Life's Symphony

I have been urged by earnest violins
And drunk their mellow sorrows to the slake
Of all my sorrows and my thirsting sins.
My heart has beaten for a brave drum's sake.
Huge chords have wrought me mighty: I have hurled
Thuds of God's thunder. And with old winds pondered
Over the curse of this chaotic world,
With low lost winds that maundered as they wandered.

I have been gay with trivial fifes that laugh;
And songs more sweet than possible things are sweet;
And gongs, and oboes. Yet I guessed not half
Life's sympathy till I had made hearts beat,
And touched Love's body into trembling cries,
And blown my love's lips into laughs and sighs.

Wilfred Owen, 1893–1918

Silent Worship

Did you not hear my lady
    Go down the garden singing?
Blackbird and thrush were silent
    To hear the alleys ringing.
O saw you not my lady
    Out in the garden there?
Shaming the rose and lily
    For she is twice as fair.

Though I am nothing to her,
    Though she must rarely look at me,
And though I could never woo her,
    I love her till I die.

Surely you heard my lady
    Go down the garden singing,
Silencing all the songbirds:
    And setting the alleys ringing,
But surely you see my lady
    Out in the garden there
Riv'ling the glittering sunshine
    With a glory of golden hair.

Ptolemy, George Frideric Handel, 1685–1759

The Music of Silence

In the highlands, in the country places,
    Where the old plain men have rosy faces,
      And the young fair maidens
          Quiet eyes;
Where essential silence cheers and blesses,
And for ever in the hill-recesses
      Her more lovely music
          Broods and dies.

O to mount again where erst I haunted;
Where the old red hills are bird-enchanted,
      And the low green meadows
          Bright with sward;
And when even dies, the million-tinted,
And the night has come, and planets glinted,
      Lo, the valley hollow
          Lamp-bestarred!

O to dream, O to awake and wander
There, and with delight to take and render,
      Through the trance of silence,
          Quiet breath;
Lo! for there, among the flowers and grasses,
Only the mightier movement sounds and passes;
      Only winds and rivers,
          Life and death.

Robert Louis Stevenson, 1850–1894

Silent Noon

Your hands lie open in the long fresh grass, –
The finger-points look through like rosy blooms:
Your eyes smile peace. The pasture gleams and glooms
'Neath billowing skies that scatter and amass.
All round our nest, far as the eye can pass,
Are golden king-cup fields with silver edge
Where the cow-parsley skirts the hawthorn hedge.
'Tis visible silence, still as the hour glass.

Deep in the sun-searched growths the dragon-fly
Hangs like a blue thread loosened from the sky: –
So this wing'd hour is dropt to us from above.
Oh! clasp we to our hearts, for deathless dower,
This close-companioned inarticulate hour
When two-fold silence was the song of love.

Dante Gabriel Rossetti, 1828–1882

Silence is not Enough

All the manifestations of the creative urge
 are but variations upon the single theme – the glory of life; –
that consummation of joy and generosity;
that magnificence and magnanimity
which is yet embodied in the simplest form, the clearest gesture.
Silence is, perhaps, the greatest hallelujah;
the silent hosannas of the sun, the stars, the trees and the flowers.
But silence is not enough – the innumerable songs of earth
mingle with the acclamations of the serene witnesses.
The wind, the water, the cries of bird and beast
and the thoughtful utterance of humanity:
each day is life's messiah
and at its feet are leaves and about its head are the canticles of joy.
Joy is met and is shared – it cannot be buried or hoarded.

William Soutar, 1898–1943

Breaking the Silence

Behold her, single in the field,
Yon solitary Highland Lass!
Reaping and singing by herself;
Stop here, or gently pass!
Alone she cuts and binds the grain,
And sings a melancholy strain;
O listen! for the Vale profound
Is overflowing with the sound.

No Nightingale did ever chaunt
More welcome notes to weary bands
Of travellers in some shady haunt,
Among Arabian sands:
A voice so thrilling ne'er was heard
In spring-time from the Cuckoo-bird,
Breaking the silence of the seas
Among the farthest Hebrides.

Will no one tell me what she sings? –
Perhaps the plaintive numbers flow
For old, unhappy, far-off things,
And battles long ago:
Or is it some more humble lay,
Familiar matter of to-day?
Some natural sorrow, loss, or pain,
That has been, and may be again?

Whate'er the theme, the Maiden sang
As if her song could have no ending;
I saw her singing at her work,
And o'er the sickle bending; –
I listened, motionless and still;
And, as I mounted up the hill,
The music in my heart I bore,
Long after it was heard no more.

William Wordsworth, 1770–1850

Everyone Sang

Everyone suddenly burst out singing;
And I was filled with such delight
As prisoned birds must find in freedom,
Winging wildly across the white
Orchards and dark-green fields;
On – on – and out of sight.
Everyone's voice was suddenly lifted;
And beauty came like the setting sun:
My heart was shaken with tears; and horror
Drifted away . . . O, but Everyone
Was a bird; and the song was wordless;
The singing will never be done.

Siegfried Sassoon, 1886–1967

The Conductor

Here is our little planet, chiefly occupied, to our view, in rushing round the sun; but perhaps found from another angle to fill quite another part in the cosmic scheme. And on this apparently unimportant speck, wandering among systems of suns, the appearance of life and its slow development and ever-increasing sensitization; the emerging of pain and of pleasure; and presently man with his growing capacity for self-affirmation and self-sacrifice, for rapture and for grief. Love with its unearthly happiness, unmeasured devotion, and limitless pain; all the ecstasy, all the anguish that we extract from the rhythm of life and death. It is much, really, for one little planet to bring to birth. And presently another music, which some – not many perhaps yet, in comparison with its population – are able to hear. The music of a more inward life, a sort of fugue in which the eternal and temporal are mingled; and here and there some, already, who respond to it. Those who hear it would not all agree as to the nature of the melody; but all would agree that it is something different in kind from the rhythm of life and death. And in their surrender to this – to which, as they feel sure, the physical order too is really keeping time – they taste a larger life; more universal, more divine. As Plotinus said, they are looking at the Conductor in the midst; and, keeping time with Him, find the fulfilment both of their striving and of their peace.

Evelyn Underhill (Mrs Stuart Moore) 1875–1941

Music and Dreams

We are the music-makers,
And we are the dreamers of dreams,
Wandering by lone sea-breakers,
And sitting by desolate streams;
World-losers and world forsakers,
On whom the pale moon gleams:
Yet we are the movers and shakers
Of the world for ever, it seems.

With wonderful deathless ditties
We build up the world's great cities.
And out of a fabulous story
We fashion an empire's glory:
One man with a dream, at pleasure,
Shall go forth and conquer a crown;
And three with a new song's measure
Can trample an empire down.

We in the ages lying
In the buried past of the earth,
Built Nineveh with our sighing,
And Babel itself with our mirth;
And o'erthrew them with prophesying
To the old of the new world's worth;
For each age is a dream that is dying,
Or one that is coming to birth.

Arthur William Edgar O'Shaughnessy, 1844–1881

*M*utual forgiveness of each vice,
Such are the Gates of Paradise.

William Blake, 1757–1827

A Hymne to God the Father

Wilt thou forgive that sinne where I begunne,
Which is my sin, though it were done before?
Wilt thou forgive those sinnes, through which I runne,
    And doe them still: though still do deplore?
        When thou hast done, thou hast not done,
           For, I have more.

Wilt thou forgive that sinne by which I'have wonne
    Others to sinne? and, made my sinne their doore?
Wilt thou forgive that sinne which I did shunne
    A yeare, or two: but wallowed in, a score?
        When thou hast done, thou hast not done,
           For, I have more.

I have a sinne of feare, that when I have spunne
    My last thred, I shall perish on the shore;
Sweare by thy selfe, that at my death thy sonne
    Shall shine as he shines now, and heretofore;
    And, having done that, Thou haste done,
           I feare no more.

John Donne, 1571 or 1572–1631

Call Christ to Mind

You have heard an insult, it is the wind;
you are angry, it is a wave.
When, therefore, the wind blows and the wave swells,
the ship is endangered,
the heart is in jeopardy,
the heart is tossed to and fro.

When you have heard an insult, you long to be avenged;
and then you are avenged,
and, rejoicing in another's harm,
find that it is you who have suffered shipwreck.
And why is this so?
Because Christ is asleep in you.

What does this mean, Christ is asleep in you?
You have forgotten Christ.
Rouse him, then, call Christ to mind,
let Christ awake in you,
give heed to him.

What did you wish? To be avenged.
Have you forgotten that when he was being crucified, he said,
'Father, forgive them, for they know not what they do?'
He who was asleep in your heart did not himself wish to be
avenged.
Wake him up, then, call him to mind . . .

What manner of man am I who wish so to be avenged?   .
I will refrain from my wrath and return to the repose of my heart.
Christ commanded the sea; tranquility is restored.

St Augustine, 354–430

A Mind Prepared

A mind prepared for red martyrdom.
A mind fortified and steadfast for white martyrdom.
Forgiveness from the heart to everyone.
Constant prayers for those who trouble thee.
Follow almsgiving before all things.
Take not of food until thou art hungry.
The love of God with all thy heart and all thy strength.
The love of thy neighbour as thyself.
Abide in God's testaments throughout all times.
Thy measure of prayer shall be until thy tears come;
or thy measure of work of labour until thy tears come.

St Columba, 521–597

Light Directed Towards God

Whenever I am in Northumbria, I think about Cuthbert. He is, even today, a much loved figure in the north, and I share with him a real love of the monastic life. Early in his life he had entered the Monastery of Melrose, and, after being there for a while, became prior . . .

He was asked to assume greater responsibilities and became prior of Holy Island. I quite easily understand how, when he was at Holy Island, he came to a crossroads in his life. He longed to be nearer to God, and his solution lay among the remote rocks, seven miles from Lindisfarne. Cuthbert became a hermit on Inner Farne, one of the Farne Islands . . . where he went to be alone with God, and to spend the whole of his time with the light in his heart directed entirely on God . . .

Throughout the history of the Church there have always been those, men and women, who have wanted to give their whole undivided attention to God . . . who turn their backs on society, not necessarily out of contempt for the world. They are totally single-minded, living out the Lord's command to watch and wait. They are a powerful witness to the primacy of the spiritual in our lives.

Basil Hume OSB, 1923–1999

Blest by Everything

I am content to follow to its source
Every event in action or in thought;
Measure the lot; forgive myself the lot!
When such as I cast out remorse
So great a sweetness flows into the breast
We must laugh and we must sing,
We are blest by everything,
Everything we look upon is blest.

William Butler Yeats, 1865–1939

The Toys

My little Son, who looked from thoughtful eyes;
And moved and spoke in quiet grown-up wise,
Having my law the seventh time disobeyed,
I struck him, and dismissed
With hard words and unkissed,
His Mother, who was patient, being dead.
Then, fearing lest his grief should hinder sleep,
I visited his bed,
But found him slumbering deep,
With darkened eyelids, and their lashes yet
From his late sobbing wet.
And I, with moan,
Kissing away his tears, left others of my own;
For, on a table drawn beside his head,
He had put, within his reach,
A box of counters and a red-veined stone,
A piece of glass abraded by the beach,
And six or seven shells,
A bottle with bluebells,
And two French copper coins, ranged there with careful art,
To comfort his sad heart.
So when that night I prayed
To God, I wept, and said:
'Ah, when at last we lie with trancèd breath,
Not vexing Thee in death,
And Thou rememberest of what toys
We made our joys,
How weakly understood
Thy great commanded good,
Then, fatherly not less
Than I whom Thou hast moulded from the clay,
Thou'lt leave Thy wrath, and say,
"I will be sorry for their childishness".'

Coventry Patmore, 1823–1896

A Dialogue between God and the Soul

Love bade me welcome: yet my soul drew back,
        Guiltie of dust and sinne.
But quick-ey'd Love, observing me grow slack
        From my first entrance in,
Drew nearer to me, sweetly questioning,
        If I lack'd any thing.

A guest, I answer'd, worthy to be here:
        Love said, You shall be he.
I the unkinde, ungratefull? Ah, my deare,
        I cannot look on thee.
Love took my hand, and smiling did reply,
        Who made the eyes but I?

Truth, Lord, but I have marr'd them: let my shame
        Go where it doth deserve.
And know you not, sayes Love, who bore the blame?
        My deare, then I will serve.
You must sit down, sayes Love, and taste my meat:
        So I did sit and eat.

George Herbert, 1593–1633

A Measure of thy Spirit

106

O Lord Jesus Christ,
give us a measure of Thy spirit
that we may be enabled to obey Thy teaching
to pacify anger,
to take part in pity,
to moderate desire,
to increase love,
to put away sorrow,
to cast away vain-glory,
not to be vindictive,
not to fear death,
ever entrusting our spirit to immortal God,
who with Thee and the Holy Ghost liveth and reigneth
world without end.

St Appollonius, died circa AD 185

Sovereign Power

Self-reverence, self-knowledge, self-control,
These three alone lead life to sovereign power.
Yet not for power (power of herself
Would come uncall'd for), but to live by law,
Acting the law we live by without fear;
And, because right is right, to follow right
Were wisdom in the scorn of consequence.

Alfred, Lord Tennyson, 1809–1892

The Shepherd Boy's Song

He that is down, needs fear no fall,
He that is low, no pride.
He that is humble, ever shall
Have God to be his guide.

I am content with what I have,
Little be it, or much:
And, Lord, contentment still I crave
Because thou savest such.

Fullness to such a burden is
That go on pilgrimage:
Here little, and hereafter Bliss,
Is best from age to age.

John Bunyan, 1628–1688

Immanence

I come in the little things,
Saith the Lord:
Not borne on morning wings
Of majesty, but I have set My feet
Amidst the delicate and bladed wheat
That springs triumphant in the furrowed sod.
There do I dwell, in weakness and in power;
Not broken or divided, saith our God!
In your strait garden plot I come to flower:
About your porch My Vine
Meek, fruitful, doth entwine;
Waits, at the threshold, Love's appointed hour.

I come in the little things,
Saith the Lord:
Yea! on the glancing wings
Of eager birds, the softly pattering feet
Of furred and gentle beasts, I come to meet
Your hard and wayward heart. In brown bright eyes
That peep from out the brake, I stand confest.
On every nest
Where feathery Patience is content to brood
And leaves her pleasure for the high emprize
Of motherhood –
There doth My Godhead rest.

I come in the little things,
Saith the Lord:
My starry wings
I do forsake,
Love's highway of humility to take:
Meekly I fit My stature to your need.
In beggar's part
About your gates I shall not cease to plead –
As man, to speak with man –
Till by such art
I shall achieve My Immemorial Plan,
Pass the low lintel of the human heart.

Evelyn Underhill (Mrs Stuart Moore), 1875–1941

Beautiful and Free

To suffer woes which Hope thinks infinite;
To forgive wrongs darker than death or nights;
To defy Power, which seems omnipotent;
To love, and bear; to Hope till Hope creates
From its own wreck the thing it contemplates;
Neither to change, nor falter, nor repent;
This, like thy glory, Titan, is to be
Good, great and joyous, beautiful and free;
This is alone Life, Joy, Empire, and Victory.

III

Percy Bysshe Shelley, 1792–1822

Discernment

God, give us grace
to accept with serenity the things that cannot be changed,
courage to change the things that should be changed,
and the wisdom to distinguish the one from the other.

Reinhold Niebuhr, 1892–1971

The prayer of the heart is the source
of all good,
which refreshes the soul as if it
were a garden.

St Gregory of Sinai, died 1360

They Planted Gardens

The cavalier gentry accepted the plain facts of existence without
questioning. Money, for instance, mattered to them a great deal.
They never married without it; they generally married to get it.
And though they felt the family bond very strongly, the closest
relations would squabble for years about the terms of a dowry or
an inheritance.

Yet they were not materialists. Their outlook was made
spiritual by the sublime background of religious belief, against
which they envisaged it. Man was an immortal soul; and his
sojourn on this planet but a brief prelude to an eternity of
eternal bliss or torment, to which he was destined according as to
how far he had attained true virtue. Their idea, too, of virtue was
exalted and spacious, appreciative of every nicety of conscience,
every impulse of magnanimity. Their hearts glowed for honour,
for chivalry, for the excellent passion of friendship, the divine
flame of love, the high mystery of virginity. With moral
sensibility went sensibility of the imagination. They delighted in
beauty. Did they not adorn themselves with velvet and lace and
lovelocks perfumed with orange flower? Their walls were rich
with carving and pictures; they wrote verses and sang them to the
lute; they planted gardens to refresh the troubled spirit; their
religion expressed itself in the jewelled and courtly mode of
George Herbert.

Lord David Cecil, 1902–1986

Thoughts in a Garden

What wondrous life is this I lead!
Ripe apples drop about my head;
The luscious clusters of the vine
Upon my mouth do crush their wine;
The nectarine and curious peach
Into my hands themselves do reach;
Stumbling on melons, as I pass,
Ensnared with flowers, I fall on grass.

Meanwhile the mind from pleasure less
Withdraws into its happiness;
The mind, that ocean where each kind
Does straight its own resemblance find;
Yet it creates, transcending these,
Far other worlds, and other seas;
Annihilating all that's made
To a green thought in a green shade.

Here at the fountain's sliding foot,
Or at some fruit-tree's mossy root,
Casting the body's vest aside,
My soul into the boughs does glide;
There, like a bird, it sits and sings,
Then whets and combs its silver wings,
And, till prepared for longer flight,
Waves in its plumes the various light.

Andrew Marvell, 1621–1678

Care Gazes Wistfully

Around my house there is an old-fashioned rambling garden,
with close-shaven grassy plots,
and fantastically clipped yews
which have gathered their darkness
from a hundred summers and winters;
and sundials in which the sun is constantly telling his age;
and statues green with neglect and the stains of the weather.
The garden I love more than any place on earth;
it is a better study than the room inside the house
which is dignified by that name.
I like to pace its gravelled walks,
to sit in the moss-house, which is warm and cosy as a bird's nest,
and wherein twilight dwells at noonday;
to enjoy the feast of colour spread for me
in the curiously shaped floral spaces.
My garden,
with its silence and the pulses of fragrance
that come and go on the airy undulations,
affects me like sweet music.
Care stops at the gates, and gazes at me wistfully through the bars.

Alexander Smith, 1830–1867

A Little More Honey in the World

It was one of the most bewitching sights in the world
to observe a hill of beans thrusting aside the soil,
or a row of early peas just peeping forth sufficiently
to trace a line of delicate green.
Later in the season the humming-birds were attracted
by the blossoms of a peculiar variety of bean;
and they were a joy to me, those little spiritual visitants,
for deigning to sip fairy food out of my nectar cups.
Multitudes of bees used to bury themselves
in the yellow blossoms of the summer-squashes.
This, too, was a deep satisfaction;
although when they had laden themselves with sweets,
they flew away to some unknown hive,
which would give back nothing in requittal
of what my garden had contributed.
But I was glad to fling a benefaction upon the passing breeze
with the certainty that somebody must profit by it,
and that there would be a little more honey in the world
to allay the sourness and bitterness
which mankind is always complaining of.

Nathaniel Hawthorne, 1804–1864

The Flower

How fresh, O Lord, how sweet and clean
Are thy returns! Ev'n as the flowers in spring;
To which, besides their own demean,
The late-past frosts tributes of pleasure bring.
                    Grief melts away
                    Like snow in May,
As if there were no such cold thing.

Who would have thought my shrivel'd heart
Could have recovered greennesse? It was gone
            Quite under ground; as flowers depart
To see their mother-root, when they have blown;
                    Where they together
                    All the hard weather,
Dead to the world, keep house unknown.

These are thy wonders, Lord of power,
Killing and quickening, bringing down to hell
            And up to heaven in an houre;
Making a chiming of a passing-bell.
                    We say amisse,
                    This or that is:
Thy word is all, if we could spell.

O that I once past changing were,
Fast in thy Paradise, where no flower can wither!
            Many a spring I shoot up fair,
Offring at heav'n, growing and groaning thither:
                    Nor doth my flower
                    Want a spring-showre,
My sinnes and I joining together:

But while I grow in a straight line,
Still upwards bent, as if heav'n were mine own,
     Thy anger comes, and I decline:
What frost to that? What pole is not the zone,
               Where all things burn,
               When thou dost turn,
     And the least frown of thine is shown?

And now in age I bud again,
After so many deaths I live and write;
     I once more smell the dew and rain,
And relish versing: O my onely light,
               It cannot be
               That I am he
     On whom thy tempests fell all night.

These are thy wonders, Lord of love,
To make us see we are but flowers that glide:
     Which when we once can finde and prove,
Thou hast a garden for us, where to bide.
               Who would be more,
               Swelling through store,
     Forfeit their Paradise by their pride.

George Herbert, 1593–1633

Fragrance and Flourish

I will heal their backsliding,
I will love them freely:
for mine anger is turned away from him.

I will be as the dew unto Israel:
he shall grow as the lily,
and cast forth his roots as Lebanon.

His branches shall spread,
and his beauty shall be as the olive tree,
and his smell as Lebanon.

They that dwell under his shadow shall return;
they shall revive as the corn, and grow as the vine:
the scent thereof shall be as the wine of Lebanon.

Hosea 14: 4–7

The Little White Rose

The Rose of all the world is not for me.
I want for my part
Only the little white rose of Scotland
That smells sharp and sweet – and breaks the heart.

Hugh MacDiarmid, 1892–1978

Happy Interruptions

I have been sitting here for an hour,
with a book on my knee,
and upon that a piece of paper
whereon I have been noting down some thoughts
for the sermon which I hope to write during this week,
and to preach next Sunday in that little parish church
of which you can see a corner of a gable
through the oaks which surround the churchyard.
I have not been able to think very connectedly, indeed;
for two little feet have been pattering round me,
two little hands pulling at me occasionally,
and a little voice entreating that I should come
and have a race upon the green.
Of course I went;
for like most men who are not very great or very bad,
I have learned,
for the sake of the little owner of the hands and the voice,
to love every little child.
Several times, too, I have been obliged to get up
and make a dash at a very small weed,
which I discerned just appearing through the gravel . . .
My sermon will be the better for these interruptions.

A K H Boyd, 1825–1899

Kail and Potatoes

As boys we ran up the brae.
As men and women, young and in our prime,
we almost forgot it was there.
But the autumn of life comes, and the brae grows steeper;
then the winter,
and once again we are as a child pausing apprehensively on the brig.
Yet we are no longer the child;
we look now for no new world at the top,
only for a little garden and a tiny house,
and a handloom in the house.
It is only a garden of kail and potatoes,
but there may be a line of daisies, white and red,
on each side of the narrow footpath,
and honeysuckle over the door.

James Matthew Barrie, 1860–1937

Bright with Holiness and Love

Make me a good gardener, O Lord.
In the garden of my life,
Let me sow the seeds of life.
Let my words be good and fruitful.
Let my ideas be sound and fertile.
Let my actions be bright with holiness and love.
As far as lies within my power,
let me sow the seeds of thy Kingdom,
and do thou, O Lord of life and growth,
make them germinate and produce
the promised harvest, O Lord of the hundredfold.

George Appleton

Frail Blossom

What are heavy? sea-sand and sorrow:
What are brief? to-day and to-morrow:
What are frail? Spring blossoms and youth:
What are deep? the ocean and truth.

Christina Georgina Rossetti, 1830–1894

The world is so full of a number
    of things,
I'm sure we should all be as
    happy as kings.

Robert Louis Stevenson, 1850–1894

Sun-rise

He who binds to himself a joy
Does the wingèd life destroy;
    But he who kisses the joy as it flies
    Lives in eternity's sun-rise.

William Blake, 1757–1827

My House

My house
Is granite
It fronts
North,

Where the Firth flows,
East the sea.
My room
Holds the first

Blow from the North,
The first from the East,
Salt upon
The pane.

In the dark
I, a child,
Did not know
The consuming night

And heard
The wind,
Unworried and
Warm – secure.

George Bruce, b. 1909

Land of Heart's Desire

I will make you brooches and toys for your delight
Of bird-song at morning and star-shine at night.
I will make a palace fit for you and me
Of green days in forests and blue days at sea.

I will make my kitchen, and you shall keep your room,
Where white flows the river and bright blows the broom,
And you shall wash your linen and keep your body white
In rainfall at morning and dewfall at night.

And this shall be for music when no one else is near,
The fine song for singing, the rare song to hear!
That only I remember, that only you admire,
Of the broad road that stretches and the roadside fire.

Robert Louis Stevenson, 1850–1894

Farther off from Heaven?

I remember, I remember,
    The house where I was born,
The little window where the sun
    Came peeping in at morn;
He never came a wink too soon,
    Nor brought too long a day,
But now, I often wish the night
    Had borne my breath away.

I remember, I remember,
    The roses, red and white;
The violets, and the lily-cups,
    Those flowers made of light!
The lilacs where the robin built,
    And where my brother set
The laburnum on his birthday –
    The tree is living yet!

I remember, I remember,
    Where I was used to swing;
And thought the air must rush as fresh
    To swallows on the wing:
My spirit flew in feathers then,
    That is so heavy now,
And summer pools could hardly cool
    The fever on my brow!

I remember, I remember,
    The fir trees dark and high;
I used to think their slender tops
    Were close against the sky:
It was a childish ignorance,
    But now 'tis little joy
To know I'm farther off from Heav'n
Than when I was a boy.

Thomas Hood, 1799–1845

A World Glittering in Tinsel

To look around in it (Haddington), one might imagine that time
had made a stand. . . But it is my native place still! and after all
there is much in it that I love. I love the bleaching-green, where I
used to caper, and roll, and tumble, and make gowan necklaces,
and chains of dandelion stalks, in the days of my *'wee existence'*;
and the schoolhouse where I carried away prizes, and signalised
myself not more for the quickness of my parts, than for the
valour of my arm, above all the boys of the community; and the
mill-dam too where I performed feats of agility which it was
easier to extol than to imitate, and which gained me at the time
the reputation of a sticket callant (un garçon assasiné) which I
believe I have maintained with credit up to the present hour; and
above all I feel an affection for a field by the side of the river,
where corn is growing now, and where a hayrick once stood –
you remember it? For my part I shall never forget that summer's
day; but cherish it *'within the secret cell of the heart'* as long as I live
– the sky was so bright, the air so balmy, the whole universe so
beautiful! I was happy then! all my little world lay glittering in
tinsel at my feet! but years have passed over it since; and storm
after storm has stript it of much of its finery – Allons ma chere!
– let us talk of the *'goosish'* man, my quondam lover.

Jane Welsh Carlyle, 1801–1866

The Glamour of Childish Days

Softly, in the dusk, a woman is singing to me;
Taking me back down the vista of years, till I see
A child sitting under the piano, in the boom of the tingling strings
And pressing the small, poised feet of a mother
    who smiles as she sings.

In spite of myself, the insidious mastery of song
Betrays me back, till the heart of me weeps to belong
To the old Sunday evenings at home, with winter outside
And hymns in the cosy parlour, the tinkling piano our guide.

So now it is vain for the singer to burst into clamour
With the great black piano appassionato. The glamour
Of childish days is upon me, my manhood is cast
Down in the flood of remembrance, I weep like a
    child for the past.

David Herbert Lawrence, 1885–1930

The Lost Island of St Kilda

I am a stranger in the crowd
I am a man upon the sea
And I must leave the city loud
And build a boat to carry me –

Beyond the Western Isles away
To live by wind and sail and hand
Three hundred miles from Mingulay
Westward, far beyond all land –

And steer for that sheer granite stack
That echoes with the seabirds' cry
And to the ruined kirk go back
Where all my fisher fathers lie

And set the rickled stones upright
Where first my mother cradled me
And crooned to us through many a night
Safe from the dark and deafening sea

I was a boy in this stark land
My barefoot youth was wild and free
Let no man seek to understand,
Whose home is not the sky and sea.

Tony Horwood

Historical footnote: In August 1929 the British Government evacuated the centuries-old but
dwindling community of St Kilda, judging that life on that remote and barren island was no
longer sustainable. The St Kildans lived out the rest of their lives on the Scottish mainland,
never ceasing to mourn their loss.

Lovely and Honourable Things

O native Britain! O my Mother Isle!
 How should'st thou prove aught else but dear and holy
To me, who from thy lakes and mountain-hills,
Thy clouds, thy quiet dales, thy rocks and seas
Have drunk in all my intellectual life,
All sweet sensations, all ennobling thoughts,
All adoration of the God in nature,
All lovely and honourable things,
Whatever makes this mortal spirit feel
The joy and greatness of its future being?
There lives nor form nor feeling in my soul
Unborrow'd from my country.

Samuel Taylor Coleridge, 1772–1834

All Beauteous Things

I love all beauteous things,
I seek and adore them;
God hath no better praise,
And man in his hasty days
Is honoured for them.

I too will something make
And joy in the making;
Although tomorrow it seem
Like empty words of a dream
Remembered on waking.

Robert Seymour Bridges, 1844–1930

Laugh and be Merry

Laugh and be merry, remember, better the world with a song,
Better the world with a blow in the teeth of a wrong.
Laugh, for the time is brief, a thread the length of a span.
Laugh, and be proud to belong to the old proud pageant of man.

Laugh and be merry: remember, in olden time,
God made heaven and earth for joy he took in a rhyme,
Made them, and filled them full with the strong red wine of his
mirth,
The splendid joy of the stars: the joy of the earth.

So we must laugh and drink from the deep blue cup of the sky,
Join the jubilant song of the great stars sweeping by,
Laugh, and battle, and work, and drink of the wine outpoured
In the dear green earth, the sign of the joy of the Lord.

Laugh and be merry together, like brothers akin,
Guesting awhile in the rooms of a beautiful inn,
Glad till the dancing stops, and the lilt of the music ends.
Laugh till the game is played; and be you merry, my friends.

John Masefield, 1878–1967

Growing Lovely, Growing Old

Let me grow lovely, growing old –
So many fine things do;
Laces, and ivory, and gold,
And silks need not be new.

And there is healing in old trees,
Old streets a glamour hold;
Why may not I, as well as these,
Grow lovely, growing old?

Karle Wilson Baker, 1878–1960

Do It!

I am only one,
But I am one.
   I cannot do everything,
   But I can do something.
      What I can do,
      I ought to do;
            And what I ought to do,
            By the grace of God I will do.

Frederic William Farrar, 1831–1903

Courtesy

Of Courtesy, it is much less
Than Courage of Heart or Holiness,
Yet in my Walks it seems to me
That the Grace of God is in Courtesy.

On monks I did in Storrington fall,
They took me straight into their Hall;
I saw Three Pictures on a wall,
And Courtesy was in them all.

The first the Annunciation;
The second the Visitation;
The third the Consolation,
Of God that was Our Lady's Son.

The first was of Saint Gabriel;
On wings a-flame from heaven he fell;
And as he went upon one knee
He shone with heavenly Courtesy.

Our Lady out of Nazareth rode –
It was her month of heavy load;
Yet was her face both great and kind,
For Courtesy was in her mind.

The third it was our little Lord,
Whom all the kings in arms adored;
He was so small you could not see
His large intent of Courtesy.

Our Lord, that was Our Lady's Son,
Go bless you, People, one by one;
My rhyme is written, my work is done.

Hilaire Belloc, 1870–1953

*L*ove is strong as death.
Many waters cannot quench love,
neither can the floods drown it.

Song of Songs 8: 6, 7

Jenny Kissed Me

Jenny kissed me when we met,
    Jumping from the chair she sat in;
Time, you thief, who love to get
    Sweets into your list, put that in!
Say I'm weary, say I'm sad,
    Say that health and wealth have missed me,
Say I'm growing old, but add,
    Jenny kiss'd me.

Leigh Hunt, 1784–1859

A Gladder Heart

My heart is like a singing bird
Whose nest is in a watered shoot;
My heart is like an apple-tree
Whose boughs are bent with thick-set fruit;
My heart is like a rainbow shell
That paddles in a halcyon sea;
My heart is gladder than all these
Because my love is come to me.

Raise me a dais of silk and down;
Hang it with vair and purple dyes;
Carve it in doves, and pomegranates,
And peacocks with a hundred eyes;
Work it in gold and silver grapes,
In leaves, and silver fleurs-de-lys;
Because the birthday of my life
Is come, my love is come to me.

Christina Georgina Rossetti, 1830–1894

To a Ladye

Sweit rois of vertew and of gentilnes,
Delitsum lyllie of everie lustynes,
Richest in bontie and in bewtie cleir,
And everie vertew that is held most deir,
Except onlie that ye ar mercyles.

In to your garthe this day I did persew,
Thair sawe I flowris that fresche wer of hew;
Baithe quhyte and reid moist lusty were to seyne,
And halsum herbis apone stalkis grene;
Yit leif nor flour fynd could I nane of rew.

I dout that Merche, with his caild blastis keyne,
Hes slene this gentill herbe that I of mene,
Quhois petewous deithe dois to my hart sic pane
That I wald mak to plant his rute agane.
So comfortand his levis unto me bene.

William Dunbar, ?1456–?1513

A Red, Red Rose

O my luve is like a red, red rose,
That's newly sprung in June.
O my luve is like the melodie,
That's sweetly played in tune.

As fair art thou, my bonnie lass,
So deep in luve am I,
And I will luve thee still, my dear,
Till a' the seas gang dry.

Till a' the seas gang dry, my dear,
And the rocks melt wi' the sun!
And I will luve thee still, my dear,
While the sands o' life shall run.

And fare thee weel, my only luve,
And fare thee weel a while!
And I will come again, my luve,
Tho' it were ten thousand mile!

Robert Burns, 1759–1796

From *Montrose to his Mistress*

My dear and only Love, I pray
    This noble World of thee,
Be govern'd by no other Sway
    But purest Monarchie.
For if Confusion have a Part,
    Which vertuous Souls abhore,
And hold a Synod in thy Heart,
    I'll never love thee more.

Like *Alexander* I will reign,
    And I will reign alone,
My Thoughts shall evermore disdain
    A Rival on my Throne.
He either fears his Fate too much,
    Or his Deserts are small,
That puts it not unto the Touch,
    To win or lose it all.

James Graham, Marquis of Montrose, 1612–1650

A Proposal

Look round with calm eyes on the persons you mention or may hereafter so mention; and if there is any one among them whose wife you had rather be – *I* do not mean whom you love better than me – but whose wife, *all* things considered, you had rather be than mine, then *I* call upon you, I your brother and husband and friend thro' every fortune, to accept that man and leave me to my destiny. But if on the contrary my heart and my hand with the barren and perplexed destiny which promises to attend them shall after all appear the best that this poor world can offer you, then take me and be content with me, and do not vex yourself with struggling to alter what is unalterable; to make a man who is poor and sick suddenly become rich and healthy.

Thomas Carlyle, 1795–1881

The Ways of Love

How do I love thee? Let me count the ways.
I love thee to the depth and breadth and height
My soul can reach, when feeling out of sight
For the ends of being and ideal grace.
I love thee to the level of every day's
Most quiet need, by sun and candlelight.
I love thee freely, as men strive for right;
I love thee purely, as they turn from praise.
I love thee with the passion put to use
In my old griefs, and with my childhood's faith.
I love thee with a love I seemed to lose
With my lost saints – I love thee with the breath,
Smiles, tears, of all my life! – and, if God choose,
I shall but love thee better after death.

Elizabeth Barrett Browning, 1806–1861

The Brightest Jewel in my Crown

O, wert thou in the cauld blast
    On yonder lea, on yonder lea,
My plaidie to the angry airt,
    I'd shelter thee, I'd shelter thee.
Or did Misfortune's bitter storms
    Around thee blaw, around thee blaw,
Thy bield should be my bosom,
To share it a', to share it a'.

Or were I in the wildest waste,
    Sae black and bare, sae black and bare,
The desert were a Paradise,
    If thou wert there, if thou wert there.
Or were I monarch of the globe,
    Wi' thee to reign, wi' thee to reign,
The brightest jewel in my crown
    Wad be my queen, wad be my queen.

Robert Burns, 1759–1796

Maud

Come into the garden, Maud,
For the black bat, night, has flown.
Come into the garden, Maud,
I am here at the gate alone;
And the woodbine spices are wafted abroad,
And the musk of the rose is blown.

For a breeze of morning moves,
And the planet of Love is on high,
Beginning to faint in the light that she loves
On a bed of a daffodil sky,
To faint in the light of the sun that she loves,
To faint in his light, and to die.

All night have the roses heard
The flute, violin, bassoon;
All night has the casement jessamine stirr'd
To the dancers dancing in tune;
Till a silence fell with the waking bird,
And a hush with the setting moon.

And the soul of the rose went into my blood,
As the music clashed in the hall;
And long by the garden lake I stood,
For I heard your rivulet fall
From the lake to the meadow and on to the wood,
Our wood, that is dearer than all;

From the meadow your walks have left so sweet
That wherever a March-wind sighs
He sets the jewel-print of your feet
In violets as blue as your eyes,
To the woody hollows in which we meet
And the valleys of Paradise.

154

The slender acacia would not shake
One long milk-bloom on the tree;
The white lake-blossom fell into the lake
As the pimpernel dozed on the lea;
But the rose was awake all night for your sake,
Knowing your promise to me;
The lilies and roses were all awake,
They sigh'd for the dawn and thee.

Alfred, Lord Tennyson, 1809–1892

Bredon Hill

In summertime on Bredon
The bells they sound so clear;
Round both the shires they ring them
In steeples far and near,
A happy noise to hear.

Here of a Sunday morning
My love and I would lie,
And see the coloured counties,
And hear the larks so high
About us in the sky.

The bells would ring to call her
In valleys miles away:
'Come all to church, good people;
Good people, come and pray.'
But here my love would stay.

And I would turn and answer
Among the springing thyme,
'Oh, peal upon our wedding,
And we will hear the chime,
And come to church in time.'

But when the snows at Christmas
On Bredon top were strown,
My love rose up so early
And stole out unbeknown
And went to church alone.

They tolled the one bell only,
Groom there was none to see,
The mourners followed after,
And so to church went she,
And would not wait for me.

156 The bells they sound on Bredon,
And still the steeples hum.
'Come all to church, good people, –'
Oh, noisy bells, be dumb;
I hear you, I will come.

Alfred Edward Houseman, 1859–1936

Proud Maisie

Proud Maisie is in the wood,
    Walking so early;
Sweet Robin sits on the bush,
    Singing so rarely.

'Tell me, thou bonny bird,
    When shall I marry me?'
'When six braw gentlemen
    Kirkward shall carry ye.'

'Who makes the bridal bed,
    Birdie, say truly?'
'The grey-headed sexton
    That delves the grave duly.'

'The glow worm o'er grave and stone
    Shall light thee steady.
The owl from the steeple sing,
    "Welcome, proud lady".'

Sir Walter Scott, 1771–1832

Comparisons

Hope is like a harebell trembling from its birth,
Love is like a rose the joy of all the earth;
Faith is like a lily lifted high and white,
Love is like a lovely rose the world's delight;
Harebells and sweet lilies show a thornless growth,
But the rose with all its thorns excels them both.

Christina Georgina Rossetti, 1830–1894

Departed Joys

Ye banks and braes o' bonnie Doon,
    How can ye bloom sae fresh and fair?
How can ye chant, ye little birds,
    And I sae weary fu' o' care!
Thou'lt break my heart, thou warbling bird,
    That wantons thro' the flowering thorn:
Thou minds me o' departed joys,
    Departed never to return.

Aft hae I roved by bonnie Doon
    To see the rose and woodbine twine;
And ilka bird sang o' its love,
    And fondly sae did I o' mine.
Wi' lightsome heart I pu'd a rose,
    Fu' sweet upon its thorny tree;
And my fause lover staw my rose –
    But ah! he left the thorn wi' me.

Robert Burns, 1759–1796

Loved, and Lost

The night has a thousand eyes,
    And the day but one;
Yet the light of the bright world dies
    With the dying sun.
The mind has a thousand eyes,
    And the heart but one;
Yet the light of a whole life dies,
    When love is done.

Francis William Bourdillon, 1852–1921

A Song through Tears

I praise Thee while my days go on;
I love Thee while my days go on:
Through dark and dearth, through fire and frost,
With emptied arms and treasure lost,
I thank Thee while my days go on.

Elizabeth Barrett Browning, 1806–1861

The Small Rain

O western wind, when wilt thou blow
    That the small rain down can rain?
Christ, if my love were in my arms,
    And I in my bed again.

Anonymous, early 16th century

As surely as I live, saith the Lord, all the earth shall be filled with the glory of God.

Numbers 14: 21

The Marvels of our World

The glory of God is present in the marvels of our world.
There is beauty to please the eye and the ear.
There is genius to be admired in the skill of the human mind
as it probes the secrets hidden within reality,
as it harnesses and controls the great powers latent within the
universe. We can adore God as the maker of all things;
we can transform humanity's inventions and skills
into hymns of praise.
To do this we need to recognise whence comes creation
and all the gifts we use
and what is the ultimate purpose of our endeavours.

Basil Hume OSB, 1923–1999

The Apple Tree

Let there be Light!
In pink and white
The apple tree blooms for our delight.
In pink and white,
Its shouts unheard,
The Logos itself, the creative Word,
Bursts from nothing; and all is stirred.
It blooms and blows and shrivels to fall
Down on the earth in a pink-white pall.
Withered? But look at each green little ball,
Crowned like a globe in the hand of God,
Each little globe in a shortening rod;
Soon to be rosy and well bestowed,
A cosmos now where the blossoms glowed
Constellated around the tree,
A cone that lifts to infinity.
Each rosy globe is as red as Mars;
And all the tree is a branch of stars.
What can we say but, 'Glory be!'
When God breaks out in an apple tree?

Oliver St John Gogarty, 1878–1957

Fulfilment

To see a world in a grain of sand
And a heaven in a wild flower
Hold Infinity in the palm of your hand
And Eternity in an hour.

William Blake, 1757–1827

All is like an Ocean

168 Lord, may I love all Thy creation,
the whole and every grain of sand in it.
May I love every leaf, every ray of Thy light.
May I love the animals:
thou hast given them the rudiments of thought and joy untroubled.
Let me not trouble it,
let me not harass them,
let me not deprive them of their happiness,
let me not work against Thine intent.
For I acknowledge unto Thee that all is like an ocean,
all is flowing and blending,
and that to withhold any measure of love
from anything in Thy universe
is to withhold that same measure from Thee.

Feodor Mikhailovich Dostoevsky, 1821–1881

Crowned with the Stars

You never enjoy the world aright,
till the Sea itself floweth in your veins,
till you are clothed with the heavens,
and crowned with the stars:
and perceive yourself to be the sole heir of the whole world,
and more than so,
because men are in it who are every one sole heirs as well as you.

Till you can sing and rejoice and delight in God,
as misers do in gold,
and Kings in sceptres,
you never enjoy the world.

Thomas Traherne, 1637–1674

The Whole Creation Join in One

170

The Lord of heav'n confess,
    On high his glory raise.
Him let all angels bless,
    Him all his armies praise.
        Him glorify,
            Sun, moon, and stars;
            Ye higher spheres,
        And cloudy sky.

From God your beings are,
    Him therefore famous make;
You all created were,
    When he the word but spake.
        And from that place,
            Where fix'd you be
            By his decree,
        You cannot pass.

Praise God from earth below,
    Ye dragons, and ye deeps:
Fire, hail, cloud, wind, and snow,
    Whom in command he keeps.
        Praise ye his name
            Hills great and small,
            Trees low and tall;
        Beasts wild and tame.

All things that creep or fly.
    Ye kings, ye vulgar throng,
All princes mean or high;
    Both men and virgins young,
        Ev'n young and old,
            Exalt his name;
            For much his fame
        Should be extoll'd.

O let God's name be prais'd
    Above both earth and sky;
For he his saints hath rais'd,
    And set their horn on high;
        Ev'n those that be
            Of Isr'el's race,
            Near to his grace.
        The Lord praise ye.

George Wither, 1588–1667

A Rainbow

My heart leaps up when I behold
A rainbow in the sky:
So was it when my life began;
So is it now I am a man;
So be it when I shall grow old,
     Or let me die!
The Child is father of the Man;
And I could wish my days to be
Bound each to each by natural piety.

William Wordsworth, 1770–1850

The Seasons

The crocus, while the days are dark,
Unfolds its saffron sheen;
At April's touch, the crudest bark
Discovers gems of green.

Then sleep the seasons, full of might;
While slowly swells the pod
And rounds the peach, and in the night
The mushroom bursts the sod.

The Winter falls: the frozen rut
Is bound with silver bars;
The snow-drift heaps against the hut,
And night is pierced with stars.

Coventry Patmore, 1823–1896

Slow Spring

O year, grow slowly. Exquisite, holy,
    The days go on
With almonds showing the pink stars blowing,
    And birds in the dawn.

Grow slowly, year, like a child that is dear,
    Or a lamb that is mild,
By little steps, and by little skips,
    Like a lamb or a child.

Katherine Tynan, 1861–1931

Another Spring

If I might see another Spring,
    I'd not plant summer flowers and wait:
I'd have my crocuses at once,
My leafless pink mezereons,
    My chill-veined snowdrops, choicer yet
    My white or azure violet,
Leaf-nested primrose; anything
To blow at once, not late.

If I might see another Spring,
    I'd listen to the daylight birds
That build their nests and pair and sing,
Nor wait for mateless nightingale;
    I'd listen to the lusty herds,
    The ewes with lambs as white as snow,
I'd find out music in the hail
And all the winds that blow.

If I might see another Spring –
    Oh stinging comment on my past
That all my past results in "if" –
If I might see another Spring
    I'd laugh to-day, to-day is brief;
    I would not wait for anything:
I'd use to-day that cannot last,
Be glad to-day and sing.

Christina Georgina Rossetti, 1830–1894

Loveliest of Trees

Loveliest of trees, the cherry now
Is hung with bloom along the bough,
And stands about the woodland ride
Wearing white for Eastertide.

Now, of my threescore years and ten,
Twenty will not come again,
And take from seventy springs a score,
It only leaves me fifty more.

And since to look at things in bloom
Fifty springs are little room,
About the woodlands I will go
To see the cherry hung with snow.

Alfred Edward Houseman, 1859–1936

Indian Summer

These are the days when birds come back,
A very few, a bird or two,
To take a backward look.

These are the days when skies put on
The old, old sophistries of June, –
A blue and gold mistake.

Oh, fraud that cannot cheat the bees,
Almost thy plausibility
Induces my belief,

Till ranks of seeds their witness bear,
And softly through the altered air,
Hurries a timid leaf!

Oh, sacrament of summer days
Oh, last communion in the haze,
Permit a child to join,

Thy sacred emblems to partake,
Thy consecrated bread to break,
Taste thine immortal wine!

Emily Dickinson, 1830–1886

Out in the Fields with God

The little cares that fretted me,
    I lost them yesterday,
Among the fields above the sea,
    Among the winds at play,
Among the lowing of the herds,
    The rustling of the trees,
Among the singing of the birds,
    The humming of the bees.

The foolish fears of what might pass
    I cast them all away
Among the clover-scented grass
    Among the new-mown hay,
Among the hushing of the corn
    Where the drowsy poppies nod,
Where ill thoughts die and good are born –
    Out in the fields with God.

Anonymous

Autumn

A touch of cold in the Autumn night –
I walked abroad,
And saw the ruddy moon lean over a hedge
Like a red-faced farmer.
I did not stop to speak, but nodded,
And round about were the wistful stars
With white faces like town children.

Thomas Ernest Hulme, 1883–1917

The Sweep of Easy Wind in Winter

Whose woods these are I think I know.
His house is in the village though:
He will not see me stopping here
To watch his woods fill up with snow.

My little horse must think it queer
To stop without a farmhouse near
Between the woods and frozen lake
The darkest evening of the year.

He gives his harness bells a shake
To ask if there is some mistake.
The only other sound's the sweep
Of easy wind and downy flake.

The woods are lovely, dark and deep.
But I have promises to keep,
And miles to go before I sleep,
And miles to go before I sleep.

Robert Frost, 1874–1963

Weathers

[I]
This is the weather the cuckoo likes,
    And so do I;
When showers betumble the chestnut spikes,
    And nestlings fly:
And the little brown nightingale bills his best,
And they sit outside at 'The Travellers' Rest,'
And maids come forth sprig-muslin drest,
And citizens dream of the south and the west,
    And so do I.

[II]
This is the weather the shepherd shuns,
    And so do I;
When beeches drip in browns and duns,
    And thresh and ply;
And hill-hid tides throb, throe on throe,
And meadow rivulets overflow,
And drops on gate-bars hang in a row,
And rooks in families homeward go,
    And so do I.

Thomas Hardy, 1840–1928

Vespers

O blackbird, what a boy you are!
How you do go it!
Blowing your bugle to that one sweet star –
How you do blow it!
And does she hear you, blackbird boy, so far?
Or is it wasted breath?
'Good Lord! She is so bright
Tonight!'
The blackbird saith.

Thomas Edward Brown, 1830–1897

The Cuckoo

Half doun the hill, whaur fa's the linn
Far frae the flaught o'fowk;
I saw upon a lanely whin
A lanely singin' gowk:
Cuckoo, cuckoo;
And at my back
The howie hill stüde up and spak:
Cuckoo, cuckoo.

There was nae soun'; the loupin' linn
Hung frostit in its fa'
Nae bird was on the lanely whin
Sae white wi' fleurs o' snaw:
Cuckoo, cuckoo:
I stude stane still;
And saftly spak the howie hill:
Cuckoo, cuckoo.

William Soutar, 1898–1943

The Donkey

When fishes flew and forests walked
    And figs grew upon thorn
Some moment when the moon was blood
    Then surely I was born.

With monstrous head and sickening cry
    And ears like errant wings,
The devil's walking parody
    On all four-footed things.

The tattered outlaw of the earth,
    Of ancient crooked will;
Starve, scourge, deride me: I am dumb,
    I keep my secret still.

Fools! For I also had my hour;
    One far fierce hour and sweet:
There was a shout about my ears,
    And palms before my feet.

Gilbert Keith Chesterton, 1874–1936

Sheep-Tracks

The tracks, the little sheep-tracks
    They wander on and on,
O'er bog and bent, and heather,
    In storm or shining weather –
It's roving down the sheep-tracks my truant heart has gone!

The tracks, the little sheep-tracks,
    They lead you God knows where:
Down by the shingle beaches
    Where mermaids comb their hair,
Over the thyme-sweet headland,
    Into the woody glen –
    Across the fairy hollow,
    I follow, follow, follow,
For the wise, the wary sheep-tracks they shun the haunts of men.

M H Noël Paton

To my Mountain

Since I must love your north
of darkness, cold, and pain,
the snow, the lovely glen,
let me love true worth,

the strength of the hard rock,
the deafening stream of wind
that carries sense away
swifter than flowing blood.

Heather is harsh to tears
and the rough moors
give the buried face no peace
but make me rise,

and oh, the sweet scent, and purple skies!

Kathleen Raine b. 1908

Silver

Slowly, silently, now the moon
Walks the night in her silver shoon;
This way, and that, she peers, and sees
Silver fruit upon silver trees;
One by one the casements catch
Her beams beneath the silvery thatch;
Couched in his kennel, like a log,
With paws of silver sleeps the dog;
From their shadowy cote the white breasts peep
Of doves in a silver-feathered sleep;
A harvest mouse goes scampering by,
With silver claws, and silver eye;
And moveless fish in the water gleam,
By silver reeds in a silver stream.

Walter de la Mare, 1873–1956

The Great Sun

I am the great sun, but you do not see me,
    I am your husband, but you turn away.
I am the captive, but you do not free me,
    I am the captain you will not obey.

I am the truth, but you will not believe me,
    I am the city where you will not stay,
I am your wife, your child, but you will leave me,
    I am that God to whom you will not pray.

I am your counsel, but you do not hear me,
    I am the lover whom you will betray,
I am the victor, but you do not cheer me,
    I am the holy dove whom you will slay.

I am your life, but if you will not name me,
Seal up your soul with tears, and never blame me.

Charles Causley, b. 1917

The Glory Passes

There was a time when meadow, grove, and stream,
     The earth, and every common sight
         To me did seem
     Apparelled in celestial light,
The glory and the freshness of a dream.
It is not now as it has been of yore: –
       Turn wheresoe'er I may,
        By night or day,
The things which I have seen I now can see no more!

     The Rainbow comes and goes,
     And lovely is the Rose;
     The Moon doth with delight
Look round her when the heavens are bare;
     Waters on a starry night
     Are beautiful and fair;
     The sunshine is a glorious birth;
     But yet I know, where'er I go,
That there hath passed away a glory from the earth

William Wordsworth, 1770–1850

Abba, Father, all things are possible unto Thee;
take away this cup from me:
nevertheless not what I will,
but what thou wilt.

The Everlasting Arms

In the course of human suffering
    the time comes
for plunging into the depths of inexpressible pain, . . .
    when human aid is of no avail:
then, more than ever before, down below conscious understanding,
    there in the unplumbed depth he waits
with open arms to receive the tortured being,
    while he infuses into the soul and mind
the absolute trust which feeds the inmost consciousness
    with the knowledge that all is well;
and with divine knowledge comes renewed strength
    to endure and lie still in the everlasting arms.

Edith Barfoot

How Suffering Takes Place

About suffering they were never wrong,
The Old Masters: how well they understood
Its human position; how it takes place
While someone else is eating or opening a window or
    just walking dully along;
How, when the aged are reverently, passionately
    waiting
For the miraculous birth, there always must be
Children who did not specially want it to happen,
    skating
On a pond at the edge of the wood:
They never forgot
That even the dreadful martyrdom must run its course
Anyhow in a corner, some untidy spot
Where the dogs go on with their doggy life and the
    torturer's horse
Scratches its innocent behind on a tree.
In Brueghel's *Icarus*, for instance: how everything
    turns away
Quite leisurely from the disaster; the ploughman may
Have heard the splash, the forsaken cry,
But for him it was not an important failure; the sun
    shone
As it had to on the white legs disappearing into the
    green
Water; and the expensive delicate ship that must have
    seen
Something amazing, a boy falling out of the sky,
Had somewhere to get to and sailed calmly on.

Wystan Hugh Auden, 1907–1973

Canadian Boat Song

Fair these broad meads – these hoary woods are grand;
But we are exiles from our fathers' land.

Listen to me, as when ye heard our father
    Sing long ago the song of other shores –
Listen to me, and then in chorus gather
    All your deep voices, as ye pull your oars.

From the lone shieling of the misty island
    Mountains divide us, and the waste of seas –
Yet still the blood is strong, the heart is Highland,
    And we in dreams behold the Hebrides.

We ne'er shall tread the fancy-haunted valley,
    Where 'tween the dark hills creeps the small clear stream,
In arms around the patriarch banner rally,
    Nor see the moon on royal tombstones gleam.

When the bold kindred, in the time long vanish'd,
    Conquer'd the soil and fortified the keep –
No seer foretold the children would be banish'd,
    That a degenerate lord might boast his sheep.

Come foreign rage – let Discord burst in slaughter!
    O then for clansman true, and stern claymore –
The hearts that would have given their blood like water
    Beat heavily beyond the Atlantic roar.

Anonymous

Egypt's Might is Tumbled Down

Egypt's might is tumbled down
    Down a-down the deeps of thought;
Greece is fallen and Troy town,
Glorious Rome hath lost her crown,
    Venice' pride is nought.

But the dreams their children dreamed
    Fleeting, unsubstantial, vain
Shadowy as the shadows seemed
Airy nothing, as they deemed,
    These remain.

Mary Elizabeth Coleridge, 1861–1907

The World is Cold

From our low seat beside the fire
Where we have dozed and dreamed and watched the glow
    Or raked the ashes, stopping so
We scarcely saw the sun or rain
    Above, or looked much higher
Than this same quiet red or burned-out fire.
    To-night we heard a call,
    A rattle on the window-pane,
    A voice on the sharp air,
And felt a breath stirring our hair,
    A flame within us: Something swift and tall
    Swept in and out and that was all.
Was it a bright or a dark angel? Who can know?
    It left no mark upon the snow,
        But suddenly it snapped the chain
        Unbarred, flung wide the door
        Which will not shut again;
And so we cannot sit here any more.
          We must arise and go:
          The world is cold without
          And dark and hedged about
          With mystery and enmity and doubt,
          But we must go
          Though yet we do not know
Who called, or what marks we shall leave upon the snow.

Charlotte Mary Mew, 1869–1928

Clouds of Glory

Our birth is but a sleep and a forgetting:
The Soul that rises with us, our life's Star,
    Hath had elsewhere its setting,
        And cometh from afar:
    Not in entire forgetfulness,
    And not in utter nakedness,
But trailing clouds of glory do we come
    From God, who is our home:
Heaven lies about us in our infancy!
Shades of the prison-house begin to close
    Upon the growing Boy,
But He beholds the light, and whence it flows,
    He sees it in his joy;
The Youth, who daily farther from the east
    Must travel, still is Nature's Priest,
    And by the vision splendid
    Is on his way attended;
At length the Man perceives it die away,
And fade into the light of common day.

William Wordsworth, 1770–1850

Triad

From the Silence of Time, Time's Silence borrow.
In the heart of To-day is the word of To-morrow.
The Builders of Joy are the Children of Sorrow.

William Sharp, 1855–1905

The Plant and Flower of Light

200

It is not growing like a tree
In bulk, doth make man better be;
Or standing long an oak, three hundred year,
To fall a log at last, dry, bald, and sere:
A lily of a day
Is fairer far in May,
Although it fall and die that night;
It was the plant and flower of light.
In small proportions we just beauties see;
And in short measures, life may perfect be.

Ben Jonson, 1572–1637

Empty Vessel

I met ayont the cairney
A lass wi' tousie hair
Singin' till a bairnie
That was nae langer there.

Wunds wi' warlds to swing
Dinna sing sae sweet,
The licht that bends owre a' thing
Is less ta'en up wi't.

Hugh MacDiarmid, 1892–1978

The Flight of a Sparrow

Such seems to me the present life of men on earth,
in comparison with that time which to us is uncertain,
as if when on a winter's night
you sit feasting with your ealdormen and thegns, –
a single sparrow should fly swiftly into the hall,
and coming in at one door, instantly fly out through another.
In that time in which it is indoors
it is indeed not touched by the fury of the winter,
but yet, this smallest space of calmness being passed almost in a
flash,
from winter going into winter again,
it is lost to your eyes.
Somewhat like this appears the life of man;
but of what follows or what went before,
we are utterly ignorant.

Venerable Bede, 673–735

My Scallop-Shell

Give me my scallop-shell of quiet,
My staff of faith to walk upon,
My scrip of joy, immortal diet,
My bottle of salvation,
My gown of Glory, hope's true gage;
And thus I'll take my pilgrimage.

Sir Walter Raleigh, 1582?–1618

O Lord,
baptize our hearts;
into a sense of the conditions and
need of all men.

George Fox, 1624–1691

All Three

I sought my God
My God I could not see;
    I sought my soul
    My soul eluded me;
        I sought my brother
        And I found all three.

The Cry of the Deer

Inasmuch . . .

You are the caller,
You are the poor,
You are the stranger at my door.

You are the wanderer,
The unfed,
You are the homeless
With no bed.

You are the Other who comes to me
To open to Another,
You are born in me.

The Cry of the Deer

Hospitality

I saw a stranger today
I put food for him in the eating-place
And drink in the drinking-place
And music in the listening-place.
In the Holy Name of the Trinity
He blessed myself and my house,
My goods and my family.
And the lark said in her warble
Often, often, often
Goes Christ in the stranger's guise
O, oft and oft and oft
Goes Christ in the Stranger's guise.

A Rune of Hospitality

No Body but Ours

We remember
that Christ has no body now on earth but ours,
no hands but ours,
no feet but ours:
ours are the eyes
through which he is to look out his compassion to the world;
ours are the feet
with which he is to go about doing good;
and ours are the hands
with which he is to bless us now.
Grant us grace to remember this
so that we may both give and receive this blessing
now and evermore.

St Theresa of Avila, 1515–1582

My Salad Days

When I was twenty one,
I pledged my life to the service of my people
and I asked God's help to make good that vow.
Although that vow was made in my salad days
when I was green in judgement,
I do not regret or retract one word of it.

Her Majesty The Queen, b. 1926

The Names of Those who Love the Lord

Abou Ben Adhem (may his tribe increase!)
Awoke one night from a deep dream of peace,
And saw within the moonlight in his room,
Making it rich, and like a lily in bloom,
An Angel, writing in a book of gold;
Exceeding peace had made Ben Adhem bold,
And to the presence in the room he said,
'What writest thou?' – The vision raised its head,
And with a look made of all sweet accord,
Answer'd, 'The names of those who love the Lord.'
'And is mine one?' said Abou. 'Nay, not so,'
Replied the angel. Abou spoke more low,
But cheerily still; and said, 'I pray thee, then,
Write me as one that loves his fellowmen.'
The angel wrote and vanish'd. The next night
It came again, with a great wakening light,
And show'd the names whom love of God had bless'd.
And, lo! Ben Adhem's name led all the rest.

Leigh Hunt, 1784–1859

Outwitted

He drew a circle that shut me out –
Heretic, rebel, a thing to flout.
But Love and I had the wit to win:
We drew a circle that took him in!

Edwin Markham, 1852–1940

Tread Softly

Had I the heavens' embroidered cloths,
Enwrought with golden and silver light,
The blue and the dim and the dark cloths
Of night and light and the half-light,
I would spread the cloths under your feet:
But I, being poor, have only my dreams;
I have spread my dreams under your feet;
Tread softly because you tread on my dreams.

William Butler Yeats, 1865–1939

*I*nto thy hands I commend my spirit: for thou hast redeemed me, O Lord, thou God of truth.

Psalm 31: 6

The Eternal Goodness

Who fathoms the eternal thought?
Who talks of scheme and plan?
The Lord is God! He needeth not
The poor device of man.

Here in the maddening maze of things,
When tossed by storm and flood,
To one fixed ground my spirit clings:
I know that God is good.

I long for household voices gone,
For vanished smiles I long;
But God hath led my dear ones on,
And he can do no wrong.

I know not what the future hath
Of marvel or surprise,
Assured alone that life and death
His mercy underlies.

And if my heart and flesh are weak
To bear an untried pain,
The bruisèd reed he will not break,
But strengthen and sustain.

And so beside the silent sea
I wait the muffled oar;
No harm from him can come to me
On ocean or on shore.

I know not where his islands lift
Their fronded palms in air;
I only know I cannot drift
Beyond his love and care.

John Greenleaf Whittier, 1807–1892

God be in my Head

218

God be in my head;
And in my understanding;
God be in myne eyes,
And in my looking;
God be in my mouth,
And in my speaking;
God be in my heart,
And in my thynking;
God be at my end,
And at my departing.

Pynson's Horae, 1514

My Soul, there is a Country

Lord, I am a countryman
coming from my country to yours.
     Teach me
     the laws of your country,
     its way of life,
     its spirit,
So that I may feel at home there.

William of Thierry, 12th century

The Long Green Grass

The life that I have is all that I have,
And the life that I have is yours.
The love that I have of the life that I have
Is yours and yours and yours.

A sleep I shall have,
A rest I shall have,
Yet death will be but a pause,
For the peace of my years in the long green grass
Will be yours and yours and yours.

Leo Marks, b. 1920

The Old Tunes

'I am playing my oldest tunes', declared she,
'All the tunes I know:
Those I learnt ever so long ago.'
Why she should think just then she'd play them
Silence cloaks like snow.

When I returned from the town at nightfall
Notes continued to pour
As when I had left two hours before.
'It's the very last time', she said in closing:
'From now I play no more.'

A few morns onward found her fading,
And, as her life outflew,
I thought of her playing her tunes right through;
And I felt she had known of what was coming
And wondered how she knew.

Thomas Hardy, 1840–1928

Dream Pedlary

If there were dreams to sell,
What would you buy?
Some cost a passing bell;
Some a light sigh,
That shakes from Life's fresh crown
Only a rose-leaf down.

If there were dreams to sell,
Merry and sad to tell,
And the crier rang the bell,
What would you buy?

A cottage lone and still,
With bowers nigh,
Shadowy, my woes to still,
Until I die.
Such pearl from Life's fresh crown
Fain would I shake me down.
Were dreams to have at will,
This would best heal my ill,
This would I buy.

Thomas Lovell Beddoes, 1803–1849

Passing the Gate

They are not long, the weeping and the laughter,
Love and desire and hate:
I think they have no portion in us after
We pass the gate.
They are not long, the days of wine and roses:
Out of a misty dream
Our path emerges for a while, then closes
Within a dream.

Ernest Dowson, 1867–1900

At Last

When on my day of life the night is falling,
    And in the winds, from unsunned spaces blown,
I hear far voices out of darkness calling
    My feet to paths unknown.

Thou who hast made my home of life so pleasant,
    Leave not its tenant when its walls decay;
O Love Divine, O Helper ever present,
    Be Thou my strength and stay.

Be near me when all else is from me drifting, –
    Earth, sky, home's pictures, days of shade and shine,
And kindly faces, to my own uplifting
    The love which answers mine.

I have but Thee, my Father; let Thy Spirit
    Be with me then to comfort and uphold;
No gate of pearl, no branch of palm I merit,
    Nor street of shining gold.

Suffice it if – my good and ill unreckoned,
    And both forgiven through Thy abounding grace –
I find myself by hands familiar beckoned
    Unto my fitting place,

Some humble door among Thy many mansions,
    Some sheltering shade where sin and striving cease,
And flows for ever, through heaven's green expansions,
    The river of Thy peace.

There, from the music round about me stealing,
    I fain would learn the new and holy song,
And find at last, beneath Thy trees of healing,
    The life for which I long.

John Greenleaf Whittier, 1807–1892

The Heavenly Country

I sigh for the heavenly country,
Where the heavenly people pass,
And the sea is as quiet as a mirror
Of beautiful, beautiful glass.

I walk in the heavenly field,
With lilies and poppies bright,
I am dressed in a heavenly coat
Of polished white.

When I walk in the heavenly parkland
My feet on the pastures are bare,
Tall waves the grass, but no harmful
Creature is there.

At night I fly over the housetops,
And stand on the bright moony beams;
Gold are all heaven's rivers,
And silver her streams.

Stevie Smith, 1902–1971

High Flight

Oh, I have slipped the surly bonds of earth
And danced the skies on laughter-silvered wings;
Sunward I've climbed and joined the tumbling mirth
Of sun-split clouds – and done a hundred things
You have not dreamed of; wheeled and soared and swung
High in the sun-lit silence. Hovering there
I've chased the shouting wind along, and flung
My eager craft through footless halls of air;
Up, up the long, delirious, burning blue
I've topped the wind-swept heights with easy grace,
Where never lark nor even eagle flew;
And while, with silent lifting mind I've trod
The high untrespassed sanctity of space,
Put out my hand, and touched the face of God.

John Gillespie Magee, 1922–1941

Crossing the Bar

Sunset and evening star,
    And one clear call for me!
And may there be no moaning of the bar,
    When I put out to sea,

But such a tide as moving seems asleep,
    Too full for sound and foam,
When that which drew from out the boundless deep
    Turns again home.

Twilight and evening bell,
    And after that the dark!
And may there be no sadness of farewell,
    When I embark;

For though from out our bourne of Time and Place
    The flood may bear me far,
I hope to see my Pilot face to face
    When I have crost the bar.

Alfred, Lord Tennyson, 1809–1892

Last Lines

No coward soul is mine,
No trembler in the world's storm-troubled sphere:
   I see Heaven's glories shine,
And Faith shines equal, arming me from Fear.

   O God within my breast,
Almighty ever-present Deity!
   Life – that in me hast rest
As I – undying Life – have power in thee!

   Vain are the thousand creeds
That move men's hearts: unutterably vain;
   Worthless as withered weeds,
Or idlest froth amid the boundless main.

   To waken doubt in one
Holding so fast by thy infinity;
   So surely anchored on
The steadfast rock of immortality.

   With wide-embracing love
Thy spirit animates eternal years,
   Pervades and broods above,
Changes, sustains, dissolves, creates, and rears.

   Though earth and man were gone,
And suns and universes ceased to be,
   And thou were left alone,
Every existence would exist in thee.

   There is not room for Death,
Nor atom that his might could render void:
   Thou – thou art Being and Breath,
And what thou art may never be destroyed.

Emily Brontë, 1818–1848

Lambs Cavorting

When I was a boy at school, a singularly silly woman was cross-
examining my headmaster about the curriculum. She wanted to
know why her son was not being taught such things as book-
keeping, accountancy, business practices, and the like. He endured
her for a while in patience; until at last she asked him point-
blank: 'In a word, Dr Alington, what *are* you preparing my son
for?' And he replied: 'In a word, Madam, for Death.'

There was more in that reply than mere wit. Paradoxically,
the one thing that is certain in this Life is Death. If we think
that, when it comes, it will clang down before us like a portcullis,
or down upon us like a guillotine, then indeed, as St Paul said,
'then is our faith vain.' But it is not only 'wishful thinking' that
makes me reject this. All my reasoning compels me to believe that
a 'creature' – in the literal sense of that word – so complicated as
I am cannot be snuffed out like a candle. Immortality may seem
unlikely; but to me anything less is not only unlikely; it is
impossible.

Each evening, from my home in the hills 300 feet above
the village of Ballantrae, I see the sun setting beyond the long
peninsula of Kintyre, knowing that it will rise again behind me
next morning over the hill of Beneraird. Every autumn, as the
days grow shorter, I know that the spring will come again with
all its welcome signs: the whaups bubbling away on the hill, the
lambs cavorting, and the larches bursting out. These are signs of
the faith which is instinctive in all of us.

Bernard Edward Fergusson, Lord Ballantrae, 1911–1980

The Last Prayer

O Domine Deus, speravi in te!
O care me Jesu, nunc libera me!

In dura catena, in misera poena,
Languendo, gemendo, et genu flectendo,
Adoro, imploro, ut liberes me!

Translation:

O Lord my God, I have hoped in Thee,
Jesus beloved, now set me free.
In harshest chain, in wretched pain,
In weakness and in sorrow sair,
Upon my knees and at my prayer,
I beg Thee that Thou freest me.

Mary, Queen of Scots, 1542–1587 (translated by Barbara Greene)

In the Face of Death

Let them bestow on ev'ry Airth a Limb;
Open all my Veins, that I may swim
To Thee my Saviour, in that Crimson Lake;
Then place my pur-boil'd Head upon a Stake;
Scatter my Ashes, throw them in the Air:
Lord (since Thou know'st where all these Atoms are)
I'm hopeful, once Thou'lt recollect my Dust,
And confident Thou'lt raise me with the Just.

James Graham, Marquis of Montrose, 1612–1650

The Death of Death

Death, be not proud, though some have called thee
Mighty and dreadful, for thou art not so:
For those whom thou think'st thou dost overthrow
Die not, poor Death; nor yet canst thou kill me.
From Rest and Sleep, which but thy pictures be,
Much pleasure, then from thee much more must flow;
And soonest our best men with thee do go –
Rest of their bones and souls' delivery.
Thou'rt slave to fate, chance, kings, and desperate men,
And dost with poison, war, and sickness dwell;
And poppy or charms can make us sleep as well
And better than thy stroke. Why swell'st thou then?
One short sleep past, we wake eternally,
And death shall be no more: Death, thou shalt die.

John Donne, 1572–1631

Safe Lodging

O Lord,
support us all the day long of this troubled life,
until the shades lengthen,
and the evening comes,
and the busy world is hushed,
the fever of life is over,
and our work is done.
Then, Lord,
in thy mercy grant us safe lodging,
a holy rest,
and peace at the last,
through Jesus Christ our Lord.

John Henry Newman, 1801–1890

A Place Prepared

234

Jesus said,
Let not your heart be troubled:
ye believe in God,
believe also in me.
In my Father's house are many mansions:
if it were not so, I would have told you.
I go to prepare a place for you.
And if I go and prepare a place for you,
I will come again,
and receive you unto myself;
that where I am, there you may be also.
Peace I leave with you,
my peace I give unto you:
not as the world giveth,
give I unto you.
Let not your heart be troubled,
neither let it be afraid.

St John 14: 1–3, 27

G od, the Father of our
    Lord Jesus Christ,
increase us in faith and truth and gentleness,
and grant us part and lot among his saints.

St Polycarp c. 69–155 AD

Heraclitus

They told me, Heraclitus, they told me you were dead,
They brought me bitter news to hear and bitter tears to shed.
I wept as I remembered how often you and I
Had tired the sun with talking and sent him down the sky.

And now that thou art lying, my dear old Carian guest,
A handful of grey ashes, long, long ago at rest,
Still are thy pleasant voices, thy nightingales, awake;
For Death, he taketh all away, but them he cannot take.

William Johnson Cory, 1823–1892

Bog Cotton

And who is to say
what they are,
rising mysterious from the loch
the wind's ripple
passing through them
their white fronds drifting.

Tethered yet free
no walls imprison them.
They spring upright after the great storm.
When winter comes they quietly disappear.

Their blossom
is soft to the touch
frail as foam.
They put a pool of light
around the longing of my heart.

And who is to say
they are not the spirits of the dead
the great and the little who lived here
Mac Gille Chaluim and his kin
rising again in the moorland of their love
their white flags tattered.

Prunella Stack, b. 1914

Friends Remembered

Oft in the stilly night
    Ere Slumber's chain has bound me,
Fond Memory brings the light
    Of other days around me;
        The smiles, the tears,
        Of boyhood's years,
    The words of love then spoken;
        The eyes that shone,
        Now dimmed and gone,
    The cheerful hearts now broken!
Thus, in the stilly night,
    Ere Slumber's chain has bound me,
Sad Memory brings the light
    Of other days around me.

When I remember all
    The friends so linked together,
I've seen around me fall,
    Like leaves in wintry weather:
        I feel like one
        Who treads alone
Some banquet-hall deserted,
        Whose lights are fled,
        Whose garland's dead,
    And all but he departed!
Thus, in the stilly night,
    Ere Slumber's chain has bound me,
Fond Memory brings the light
    Of other days around me.

Thomas Moore 1779–1852

Precious Friends

When to the sessions of sweet silent thought
I summon up remembrance of things past,
I sigh the lack of many a thing I sought,
And with old woes new wail my dear times' waste:
Then can I drown an eye, unus'd to flow,
For precious friends hid in death's dateless night,
And weep afresh love's long since cancell'd woe,
And moan the expense of many a vanish'd sight:
Then can I grieve at grievances foregone,
And heavily from woe to woe tell o'er
The sad account of fore-bemoaned moan,
Which I new pay as if not paid before.
       But if the while I think on thee, dear friend,
       All losses are restor'd and sorrows end.

William Shakespeare 1564–1616

Jewels in my Hand

I hold dead friends like jewels in my hand
Watching their brilliance gleam against my palm
Turquoise and emerald, jade, a golden band.

All ravages of time they can withstand
Like talismans their grace keeps me from harm
I hold dead friends like jewels in my hand.

I see them standing in some borderland
Their heads half-turned, waiting for my arm
Turquoise and emerald, jade, a golden band.

I'm not afraid they will misunderstand
My turning to them like a magic charm
I hold dead friends like jewels in my hand
Turquoise and emerald, jade, a golden band.

Sasha Moorsom, 1931–1993

The Comfort of Friends

They that love beyond the world cannot be separated by it.
Death cannot kill what never dies.
Nor can spirits ever be divided
that love and live in the same Divine Principle,
the root and record of their friendship.
If absence be not death, neither is theirs.
Death is but crossing the world, as friends do the seas;
they live in one another still.
For they must needs be present,
that love and live in that which is omnipresent.
In this divine glass, they see face to face;
and their converse is free, as well as pure.
This is the comfort of friends,
that though they may be said to die,
yet their friendship and society are, in the best sense, ever present,
because immortal.

William Penn, 1644–1718

The Truly Great

I think continually of those who were truly great.
Who, from the womb, remembered the soul's history
Through corridors of light where the hours are suns
Endless and singing. Whose lovely ambition
Was that their lips, still touched with fire,
Should tell of the Spirit clothed from head to foot in song.
And who hoarded from the Spring branches
The desires falling across their bodies like blossoms.

What is precious is never to forget
The essential delight of the blood drawn from ageless springs
Breaking through rocks in worlds before our earth.
Never to deny its pleasure in the morning simple light
Nor its grave evening demand for love.
Never to allow gradually the traffic to smother
With noise and fog the flowering of the spirit.

Near the snow, near the sun, in the highest fields
See how these names are fêted by the waving grass
And by the streamers of white cloud
And whispers of wind in the listening sky.
The names of those who in their lives fought for life
Who wore at their hearts the fire's centre.
Born of the sun they travelled a short while towards the sun,
And left the vivid air signed with their honour.

Stephen Spender, b. 1909

The Gladness of the World

O may I join the choir invisible
Of those immortal dead who live again
In minds made better by their presence: live
In pulses stirred to generosity,
In deeds of daring rectitude, in scorn
For miserable aims that end with self,
In thoughts sublime that pierce the night like stars,
And with their mild persistence urge man's search
To vaster issues . . .
                              This is life to come,
Which martyred men have made more glorious
For us who strive to follow. May I reach
That purest heaven, be to other souls
The cup of strength in some great agony,
Enkindle generous ardour, feed pure love,
Beget the smiles that have no cruelty –
Be the sweet presence of a good diffused,
And in diffusion ever more intense.
So shall I join the choir invisible
Whose music is the gladness of the world.

George Eliot, 1819–1880

Pack up the Moon

Stop all the clocks, cut off the telephone,
Prevent the dog from barking with a juicy bone,
Silence the pianos and with muffled drum
Bring out the coffin, let the mourners come.

Let aeroplanes circle moaning overhead
Scribbling on the sky the message He Is Dead,
Put the crêpe bows round the white necks of the public doves,
Let the traffic policemen wear black cotton gloves.

He was my North, my South, my East and West,
My working week and my Sunday rest,
My noon, my midnight, my talk, my song;
I thought that love would last for ever: I was wrong.

The stars are not wanted now: put out every one;
Pack up the moon and dismantle the sun;
Pour away the ocean and sweep up the wood.
For nothing now can ever come to any good.

Wystan Hugh Auden 1907–1973

'Gone On'

We can no longer see you
You make no sound.
The world believes you have 'gone on'
      somewhere.
Theories abound.

Where could you go,
our lively, lovely friend?
For God is the life of man
without start or end.

God holds His world complete,
in its life we share,
there is nowhere out of this world to go:
no here or there.

Ours, only ours the blindness,
ours is the road to take
(through the mists and the myths and the
      laws that part
and the hearts that break).

Into that still, small place
where illusion's done
and we find that you, us, and all
with God are one.

Virginia Thesiger, 1910–1993

Only an Horizon

We seem to give them back to thee, O God,
who gavest them to us.
Yet as thou did'st not lose them when thou gavest them to us,
so we do not lose them by their return.
Not as the world giveth, givest thou, O lover of souls.
What thou givest, thou takest not away,
for what is thine is ours also if we are thine.
And life is eternal and love is immortal,
and death is only an horizon,
and an horizon is nothing save the limit of our sight.
Lift us up, strong Son of God,
that we may see further;
cleanse our eyes that we may see more clearly;
draw us closer to thyself,
that we may know ourselves to be nearer to our loved ones
who are with thee.
And while thou dost prepare a place for us,
prepare us also for that happy place,
that where thou art there we may be also for evermore. Amen.

Variously attributed to Anonymous, William Penn, 1644–1718,
and Bede Jarrett, 1881–1934

Remember

Remember me when I am gone away,
Gone far away into the silent land;
When you can no more hold me by the hand,
Nor I half turn to go yet turning stay.
Remember me when no more day by day
You tell me of our future that you planned:
Only remember me; you understand
It will be late to counsel then or pray.
Yet if you should forget me for a while
And afterwards remember, do not grieve:
For if the darkness and corruption leave
A vestige of the thoughts that once I had,
Better by far you should forget and smile
Than that you should remember and be sad.

Christina Georgina Rossetti, 1830–1894

Forgive if I Forget

Cold in the earth – and the deep snow piled above thee,
Far, far removed, cold in the dreary grave!
Have I forgot, my only Love, to love thee,
Severed at last by Time's all-severing wave?

Cold in the earth – and fifteen wild Decembers
From those brown hills have melted into spring:
Faithful indeed is the spirit that remembers
After such years of change and suffering!

Sweet Love of youth, forgive if I forget thee
While the world's tide is bearing me along;
Other desires and other hopes beset me,
Hopes which obscure, but cannot do thee wrong!

No later light has lightened up my heaven;
No second morn has ever shone for me:
All my life's bliss from thy dear life was given,
All my life's bliss is in the grave with thee.

But, when the days of golden dreams had perished,
And even Despair was powerless to destroy,
Then did I learn how existence could be cherished,
Strengthened, and fed without the aid of joy;

Then did I check the tears of useless passion,
Weaned my young soul from yearning after thine;
Sternly denied its burning wish to hasten
Down to that tomb already more than mine.

And, even yet, I dare not let it languish,
Dare not indulge in Memory's rapturous pain;
Once drinking deep of that divinest anguish,
How could I seek the empty world again?

Emily Brontë, 1818–1848

The Spring Begins

For winter's rains and ruins are over,
And all the season of snows and sins;
The days dividing lover and lover,
    The light that loses, the night that wins;
And time remembered is grief forgotten,
And frosts are slain, and flowers begotten,
And in green underwood and cover
    Blossom by blossom the spring begins.

Algernon Charles Swinburne, 1837–1909

Auld Lang Syne

Should auld acquaintance be forgot,
    And never brought to mind?
Should auld acquaintance be forgot,
    And auld lang syne?

For auld lang syne, my jo,
    For auld lang syne,
We'll tak a cup o' kindness yet,
    For auld lang syne.

And surely you'll be your pint-stowp,
    And surely I'll be mine,
And we'll tak a cup o kindness yet
    For auld syne!

We twa hae run about the braes,
    And pu'd the gowans fine,   *daisies*
But we've wandered mony a weary fit
    Sin' auld lang syne.

We twa hae paidled in the burn,   *paddled*
    Frae morning sun till dine,
But seas between us braid hae roared
    Sin' auld lang syne.

And there's a hand, my trusty fiere,   *comrade*
    And gie's a hand o' thine;
And we'll tak a right guid-willie waught, *hearty draught*
    For auld lang syne!

Robert Burns, 1759–1796

Weep No More

Do not stand at my grave and weep

  I am not there.

  I do not sleep.

I am a thousand winds that blow

I am the diamond glints on snow.

I am the sunlight on ripened grain

I am the gentle autumn rain.

When you awaken in the morning's hush,

I am the swift uplifting rush

  Of quiet birds

  in circled flight.

I am the soft stars that shine at night.

Do not stand at my grave and cry,

  I am not there;

  I did not die.

Anonymous

Uncle Vanya

SONIA [*comes back and puts the candle on the table*]. He's gone.
VOINITSKY (UNCLE VANYA) [*counts on the abacus and writes down*].
Total fifteen. twenty-five.
MARINA [*yawns*]. Lord forgive us our sins.
[TELYEGHIN *enters on tiptoe, sits down by the door and quietly tunes his guitar.*]
VOINITSKY [*to Sonia, passing his hand over her hair*]. My child, there's
such a weight on my heart! Oh, if only you knew how my heart aches!
SONIA. Well, what can we do? We must go on living! [*A pause.*] We
shall go on living, Uncle Vanya. We shall live through a long, long
succession of days and tedious evenings. We shall patiently suffer the
trials which Fate imposes on us; we shall work for others, now and in
our old age, and we shall have no rest. When our time comes we shall
die submissively, and over there, beyond the grave, we shall say that
we've suffered, that we've wept, that we've had a bitter life, and God
will take pity on us. And then, Uncle dear, we shall both begin to
know a life that is bright and beautiful, and lovely. We shall rejoice and
look back at these troubles of ours with tender feelings, with a smile –
and we shall have rest. I believe it, Uncle, I believe it fervently, passion-
ately. [*Kneels before him and lays her head on his hands, in a tired voice.*] We
shall have rest!
[TELYEGHIN *plays softly on the guitar.*]
SONIA We shall rest! We shall hear the angels, we shall see all the
heavens covered with stars like diamonds, we shall see all earthly evil,
all our sufferings swept away by the grace which will fill the whole
world, and our life will become peaceful, gentle, and sweet as a caress. I
believe it, I believe it ... [*Wipes his eyes with her handkerchief.*] Poor, poor
Uncle Vanya, you're crying. [*Tearfully.*] You've had no joy in your life,
but wait, Uncle Vanya, wait. We shall rest. [*Embraces him.*] We shall rest!
[*The watchman taps.*]
[MARYIA VASSILIEVANA *makes notes on the margin of her pamphlet,*
MARINA *knits her stocking.*]
SONIA. We shall rest!
the curtain drops slowly

Anton Pavlovich Chekhov, 1860–1904

Notes on Sources and Authors

The compilers are grateful to all whose work appears in this volume. They ask pardon for any inadvertent infringement of copyright that may have been committed. They also acknowledge with heartfelt thanks their indebtedness to a variety of sources for much of the material for the following notes, chief among them such reference works as *The Dictionary of National Biography*, *The Oxford Companion to English Literature, Fourth Edition* edited by Sir Paul Harvey, 1967; and *The Mainstream Companion to Scottish Literature* by Trevor Royle, 1993. They would be pleased to be notified about material which is used here but has not been acknowledged, and will rectify such omissions in any future printings.

Page
number

p. v   *Poems by Ann Lyon* Faber & Faber 1937 epigraph.

1.   'The Inward Light ...' *Quaker Faith and Practice* © The Yearly Meeting of the Religious Society of Friends (Quakers) in Britain, 1995 Printed by Warwick Printing Company Limited Section 19.24. George Fox, the son of a Leicester weaver, was the founder of the Society of Friends, at first called 'The Children of Light', subsequently 'Friends of Truth' or 'Truth's Friends', happily abbreviated to 'Friends'. The more common name, 'Quakers', was first used at Derby on 30 October, 1650, when Fox and his colleague Fretwell were before the magistrates. Fox told them to 'tremble at the word of the Lord, whereupon one of the magistrates, Gervasse Bennet, "retorted upon them the name of quakers"'. Fox became an itinerant missionary for his cause, travelling into almost every corner of England and Wales, to Scotland, Ireland, the West Indies, North America, and Holland. He suffered imprisonment eight times, but remained undaunted to the end.

3.   *The Church Hymnary: Third Edition* no. 474 (verses 4 and 5 [the original has Church in verse 5, not world]) Oxford University Press 1973. George Kennedy Allen Bell, Bishop of Chichester, gave distinguished service to the ecumenical movement, and presided over the World Council of Churches.

4.   *On the Gospel of John, 34, 3* in *Prayers of St Augustine* Barry Ulanov Seabury Press, Minneapolis, Minnesota, 1983 p. 27. Though the influence of his mother, St Monica, was to prove formative in the development of St Augustine's Christian experience, it was not until he met St Ambrose of Milan that he was able to embrace the doctrines and discipline of the Christian faith in all their fullness. He was baptized in 387, ordained priest in 391, and consecrated Bishop of Hippo in 395. His voluminous writings became almost the staple of the medieval Church and continue to exert their influence still.

5.   *A Diary of Private Prayer* John Baillie, Oxford University Press 1936 p. 33. John Baillie was Professor of Divinity in the University of Edinburgh 1934–56, and was Moderator of the General Assembly of the Church of Scotland in 1943. He

and his brother Donald (professor in St Andrews University) were theologians of international repute: they dominated Scottish theology in the middle decades of the twentieth century.

6. Eastern Church. Quoted in *God of a Hundred Names* Barbara Greene and Victor Gollancz, Victor Gollancz Limited 1962 p. 28.

7. St Dimitrii of Rostov Quoted in *The Oxford Book of Prayer* Editor: George Appleton Oxford University Press 1985 p. 4; taken from The Orthodox Way Bishop Kallistos Ware Mowbray & Co. Ltd

8. *A Child's Garden of Verses* Robert Louis Stevenson. Facsimile edition Mainstream 1990 p. 55. Robert Louis Stevenson, novelist, essayist, poet, and traveller, has in this book given to the world what many regard as some of the greatest recollections of childhood. See p. 64 *infra*.

9. *The Commonweal* Algernon Charles Swinburne *Complete Poetical Works* Heinemann. Swinburne was the master of melodious verse, and a dramatist of perception and power. His large body of writing (literary criticism, biographical monograms, and articles for the *Encyclopaedia Britannica* as well as poetry) includes three romantic dramas on the subject of Mary Queen of Scots.

10. *Zorba the Greek* Nikos Kazantzakis translated by Carl Wildman, Faber and Faber, London and Boston 1961 p. 119.

11. From *Hymns of Faith and Hope* 1861, as it appears in *The Church Hymnary: Third Edition* Oxford University Press no. 131. Horatius Bonar was one of the leading ministers of the Free Church of Scotland, and the most important Scottish hymn-writer of the nineteenth century. He is buried in Canongate Kirkyard.

12. *Prayer for his Fellow Prisoners, Christmas 1943* in *Letters and Papers from Prison* Dietrich Bonhoeffer, SCM Press Ltd. As a lecturer in systematic theology in the University of Berlin in the 1930's, Bonheoffer attacked Hitler's political ideas. He was first forbidden to teach, then banned from Berlin by the Nazi authorities. He was arrested, imprisoned in Buchenwald in 1943, and executed in Flossenburg in 1945.

13. *Common Order 1994* St Andrew Press 1994 p. 72. *Common Order* is the most recent Service Book of the Church of Scotland.

14. *Drawing Near the Light in Poems by the Way* William Morris, Longmans Green 1891. William Morris was notable in his day not only as a poet and artist, but also (and often in collaboration with Rossetti, Burne-Jones, and Madox Brown) as a decorator, manufacturer, and printer.

15. *The Other Landscape* Neil Miller Gunn, Richard Drew Publishing, Glasgow 1988 p. 13. Neil Gunn was one of Scotland's most distinguished twentieth century writers, describing not only the landscape and history of Scotland but also the high and low points of the human spirit's mystical quest.

16. *The Night in Silex Scintillans Part 2 1655* Henry Vaughan, physician and poet, was influenced by the mystical occultism of his time, fascinated by the imagery and teaching of the Bible, and, in this poem, inspired by George Herbert.

17. *Church Hymnary: Third Edition* Oxford University Press 1973 no. 34. This poem by Oliver Wendell Holmes, Professor of Anatomy at Harvard, first appeared in *The Atlantic Monthly*, 1859, at the end of his *Professor at the Breakfast Table*, with this introduction: 'Peace to all such as may have been vexed in spirit by any utterance these pages may have repeated! They will doubtless forget for the moment the difference in the hues of truth we look at through our human prisms, and join in singing (inwardly) this hymn to the source of the light we all need to lead us, and the warmth which alone can make us all brothers.'

18. Henry Vaughan. see p. 16 *supra*.

19. This sentence is quoted in *God of a Hundred Names* Barbara Greene and Victor Gollancz Victor, Gollancz 1962 p. 45 William Penn was a politician, courtier, and theologian, a prolific writer, and the founder of the Colony of Pennsylvania, where he lived for just four years. He hailed from Buckinghamshire and was a frequent attender at the Meeting House in Jordans near Amersham and was buried in its grounds in 1718. Simon Jenkins in his *England's Thousand Best Churches* (Allen Lane The Penguin Press 1999 p. 31) calls Jordans the Quaker Westminster Abbey, and recalls how the authorities in Pennsylvania sought to have his remains reburied in the State Capital. On one occasion two men had to be stopped from trying to exhume them. The Friends expressed the view that such a removal to America 'amid the pomp and circumstance of a state ceremonial accompanied in all probability by military honours and parade, would be utterly repugnant to his [Penn's] known character and sentiments.' And that was that.

21. The epigraph in *The Quiet Heart* George Appleton Collins (Fount) 1983 preface. For a note about Evelyn Underhill, see p. 94 *infra*.

22. The compilers have no information to hand about Bishop Palmer.

23. *At Night* in *Poems of Alice Meynell* Burns Oates & Washbourne Ltd London 1927 p. 144. Alice Meynell was a wife and mother (eight children) who still found time to make a substantial and enduring contribution to literature by her poetry, essays, and journalism.

24. Source unknown.

25. This Invocation is used at the opening of the annual Eisteddfod in Wales, and was translated by the Recorder of the Gorsedd, B G Evans.

26. *The Hero as a Man of Letters* in *On Heroes, Hero-Worship, and the Heroic in History* Thomas Carlyle, Chapman and Hall, Chelsea edition, 1841, Lecture V, p. 301. No writer was more influenced by his antecedents and surroundings than Thomas Carlyle. He was a Scot to the marrow. He was born in Ecclefechan in Dumfries-

shire, brought up in Annandale, and lived for about five years after his marriage in the family home of his wife Jane Welsh at Craigenputtoch on the lonely moors of Nithsdale. He spent much of his mature life, however, in Chelsea where he was capable of judging London society with the same searing severity as Knox judged the court of Mary, Queen of Scots. The tone of his writings perhaps owed as much to his roots in Scottish Calvinism, as it did to the dyspepsia which, he claimed, was like 'a rat gnawing at the pit of his stomach'.

27. *Poems of Alice Meynell* Burns Oates & Washbourne Ltd London 1927 p. 51. See p. 23 *supra*.

28. Is this St Isaias one of the five Egyptian brothers who went to visitm the Christians condemned to the mines in Cilicia, and were tortured and beheaded under the Emperor Diocletian?

29 *God of a Hundred Names* Barbara Greene and Victor Gollancz, Victor Gollancz 1962 p. 44. St Clement comes early in the list of Bishops of Rome; he may have been a disciple of St Peter and of St Paul. His writings were formative for the early Church.

31. *God of a Hundred Names* Barbara Greene and Victor Gollancz, Victor Gollancz 1962 p. 45. This lovely poem is the fruit of a young life cut short: D M Dolben was drowned at Oxford, where he was a contemporary of Robert Bridges.

32. *The Excursion* Book IV l. 1133 William Wordsworth *The Poetical Works of Wordsworth* Edited by Thomas Hutchison, Revised by Ernest de Selincourt Oxford University Press 1936 p. 818. In 1813, at the age of 43, William Wordsworth was given the office of distributer of stamps for the county of Westmorland, for which he was paid £400 a year. This was his first 'real' job: before then, he had attended university; spent time on walking tours in France, Italy, and Scotland; struck up friendships with Coleridge and Sir Walter Scott; married Mary Hutchinson of Penrith; and published many poems and critical articles. For income, he had depended largely on his literary work, helped occasionally by legacies and gifts. Now, with the salary from his public office, he was more financially secure. The poems flowed from his new home, Rydal Mount, in Grasmere; the tours and travelling continued; and his fame increased. He resigned his office in 1842 and received a pension from the civil list. He was appointed poet laureate in 1843 in succession to Robert Southey.

33. This verse by Joseph Campbell, an Irish poet, is often sung to a male voice choir setting by Hugh S Roberton.

34. *Missale ad Usum Sarum* was used widely in Scotland, as well as in England, before the Reformation.

35. *Confessions 10, xxvii, 38* in *Prayers of St Augustine* Barry Ulanov Seabury Press, Minneapolis, Minnesota, 1983 p. 70. See p. 4 *supra*.

36. *Contemporary Prayers for Public Worship*, 1967 p. 48. This book of prayers was prepared by Congregationalist Ministers after the Nottingham Faith and Order Conference in 1964. Dr Caryl Micklem, who edited the book, was Minister of Kensington Chapel, London.

37. *The White Peace* by William Sharp, in *The Oxford Book of Mystical Verse* chosen by D H S Nicholson and A H E Lee, 1917 Oxford University Press p. 398. William Sharp was educated at Glasgow Academy and Glasgow University. He wrote, under his own name, lives of D G Rossetti, P B Shelley, and R Browning, and several other works; but when he came to write mystical prose and verse, he adopted the name 'Fiona MacLeod'. His identity with 'Fiona MacLeod' was not known until after his death.

38. In *The Church Hymnary: Third Edition* Oxford University Press 1973 no. 76. John Greenleaf Whittier (Haverhill, Massachusetts) began life as a farm boy and a slipper-maker. He bought a copy of Robert Burns's works from a pedlar, whose singing of the songs of the Ayrshire poet so thrilled the lad that he began to experiment in verse himself. His verses found their way into newspapers, and he eventually became a journalist, writing powerfully against slavery. He was a member of the Society of Friends, and to the last wore their distinctive garb and used their mode of speech.

39. *Poems of Ivar Campbell with Memoir by Guy Ridley*. Printed by A L Humphreys, 187 Piccadilly, London 1917 p. 35. Ivar Campbell was the only son of Lord George Campbell, RN, who was the fourth son of the eighth Duke of Argyll. The Duke, who served in Gladstone's cabinet, was famed as an orator. At the beginning of the First World War, Ivar, his grandson, went to enlist in the army, but failed his medical test due to trouble with his eyesight. Deeply disappointed, he decided to keep a book shop in Chelsea where, under the name of Mr John Cowslip, he sold books, drawings by modern artists, and holly walking-sticks. He had a remarkable empathy with children, and it was mutual. Eventually, he passed his medical and was given a Commission in the Argyll and Sutherland Highlanders. On receiving the news, he sent a telegram to his parents: 'Passed Medical. Home for dinner. Kill the fatted calf.' After serving in France, he sailed east with his regiment. They pitched camp in the wilderness of Mesopotamia. An attack was launched against a strong Turkish position. Ivar Campbell was mortally wounded whilst leading his men in this engagement, and died the next day. He was buried by the banks of the Tigris. He was in his twenty-sixth year when he died.

40. *Heaven-Haven* has the sub-title *A Nun takes the Veil*. Gerard Manley Hopkins numbered Bridges, Dolben, and Coventry Patmore among his friends, and, after his conversion to the Church of Rome in 1868, Newman as well. He became a Jesuit novitiate in 1868, and was appointed to the Chair of Greek at Dublin University in 1884. His poems were collected and published posthumously by Robert Bridges, in 1918. An enlarged edition was edited by W H Gardner and N H Mackenzie in 1967.

41. From *La Messe Sur Le Monde* Pierre Teilhard de Chardin, S J Collins. Teilhard de Chardin was at once a biologist, paleontologist, and a Jesuit Father. His name was a byword in international scientific circles. He spent a good deal of his life in China where he played a major role in the discovery of Peking Man in 1929. His abiding passion was to attempt to reconcile Christian theology with the natural sciences, a task he achieved with a poetry of vision which makes him eloquent still today.

42. *The Island Sanctuary* by M H Noël Paton first appeared in *A Wanderer's Lute* Alexander Moring Ltd, London, but, for this book, it is taken from *A Hebridean Medley*, which was privately printed by Macrae & Patterson, 96 Nicolson Street, Edinburgh, p. 11.

43. From *St Francis of Assisi Omnibus of Sources: Early Writings and Early Biographies*, edited by Marion A Habig OFM. Copyright 1973 Franciscan Herald Press, 1434 W. 51st Street Chicago, IL 60609. St Francis is credited with being the first to write hymns in the vernacular: it is fitting, therefore, that this well-loved prayer of his now appears in many hymn books as a hymn.

44. In *The Church Hymnary: Third Edition* Oxford University Press no. 675. This hymn first appeared as a poem in *Glen Desseray and other Poems* in 1888. John Campbell Shairp was at once the Principal of St Andrews University and the Professor of Poetry at Oxford – a curious, and probably unique, combination.

45. *The Hero as a Man of Letters* in *On Heroes, Hero-Worship, and the Heroic in History* Thomas Carlyle, Chapman and Hall, Chelsea edition, 1841, Lecture V, p. 339. See p. 26 *supra*.

47. *The Secret* R S Cushman from *Spiritual Hilltops* 1932 Abingdon Press.

48. *Just for Today* Sybil F Partridge, from *Prayer for the Day*, Selections from the BBC radio programme, compiled by Hope Sealy. In the broadcast programme, this poem was sung by Robert White, the Irish-American tenor.

50. *The Church Hymnary: Third Edition* Oxford University Press no. 574. Reginald Heber, Bishop of Calcutta, did much to popularize the use of hymns in England. In 1811 he began to publish his own hymns in *The Christian Observer*, and in collaboration with Dean Milman he made the first attempt to provide a set of hymns adapted to the requirements of the Christian Year. These were published in 1827 as *Hymns written and adapted to the Weekly Church Service of the Year*. This short communion hymn is one of these.

51. *Church Hymnary: Third Edition* Oxford University Press no. 580. William Bright was theological tutor at Glenalmond College, Perthshire, and Canon of Cumbrae Cathedral before becoming Regius Professor of Ecclesiastical History at Christ Church, Oxford, where he also became a Canon. His hymn for Holy Communion was published in *The Monthly Packet* 1873.

52. This version of Psalm 84, much loved throughout Scotland, first appeared in the *Scottish Psalter* of 1650, and is printed in the *Scottish Psalter*, 1929, Oxford University Press. It is commonly sung to the tune *Harrington*.

53. From *The Administration of the Communion in The Liturgy and other Divine Offices of the Church* 1910, which was the Service Book of the Catholic Apostolic Church. The Services of the Catholic Apostolic Church were full of ritual and symbolism, and their rich liturgy has proved to be a valuable quarry for the twentieth century Church at large. The Liturgy owes much to Edward Irving (1792–1834), a minister of the Church of Scotland who was excommunicated in 1833. He was a close friend of Thomas Carlyle.

54. *Psalm 96: 6–9* in the *Authorised Version* of the *Holy Bible 1611*.

55. *The Poetical Works of George Macdonald* Chatto & Windus 1911 vol 2 p. 160. George Macdonald was notable in his day as a novelist and poet and man of letters. He is now best remembered for his children's books and what C.S Lewis called his 'mythopœic art', both of which had a lasting influence on Lewis.

56. From *Readings in St John's Gospel* William Temple, Macmillan and Co., Ltd 1952. It may fairly be claimed that William Temple was the greatest of the twentieth century Archbishops of Canterbury. His deep spirituality was matched by a passion for social and national righteousness, and his tireless work for the union of the Churches marched hand in hand with a determination to provide a reasoned exposition of the Christian faith.

57. *Ezekiel 34: 25, 26* in the *Authorised Version* of the *Holy Bible* 1611.

59. Although attributed to St Columba, the source of this Blessing remains unknown.

60. From the Second Morning Service in *The Book of Common Order* Oxford University Press 1940 p. 19.

61. *Susan Coolidge* was the pseudonym for Sarah Chauncey Woolsey who was born in Cleveland, Ohio, edited books of verse and the letters of Jane Austen and Fanny Burney, and wrote the Katy books.

62. *Sermon, 241, ii, 2* in *Prayers of St Augustine*. Barry Ulanov, Seabury Press, Minneapolis, Minnesota, 1983 p. 43. See p. 4 *supra*.

63. From *100 Second Best Poems* chosen by C Lewis Hind, A M Philpot, London 1925 p. 67. Henry Wadsworth Longfellow, American poet and professor at Harvard, is perhaps best known for his *Hiawatha*, a somewhat curious poem written in trochaic dimeters. It reproduces American Indian stories which centre on Hiawatha (there was a real Mohawk chief of that name, a statesman and a reformer) who married Minnehaha, ' Laughing Water', the Dacotah maiden. But Longfellow's output was considerable and notable, some of it deeply serious and reflecting something of the sadness that shadowed his life: his first wife died while they were on holiday in Holland, and his second wife was burnt to death.

64. This is part of the first prayer in *Prayers written at Vailima* Robert Louis Stevenson, illuminated by Alberto Sangorski, Chatto & Windus. Robert Louis Stevenson came from a family of lighthouse builders. He himself studied engineering at Edinburgh University, but he turned to the law and became an advocate at the Scottish Bar. His real love, however, was writing, which he pursued in spite of precarious health. In 1888, he settled at Vailima in Samoa where he temporarily recovered his health. But he died there suddenly, and was buried there by the Samoans who revered him as 'Tusi-tala', the teller of tales. Family Prayers, composed and conducted by Stevenson, were part of the order of the day at Vailima: the prayer quoted here is the first of these prayers.

66. *Numbers 6: 24–27* in the *Authorised Version* of the *Holy Bible* 1611.

67. *The Hebridean Altars: Some Studies of the Spirit of an Island Race* Alistair Maclean Moray Press 1937 p. 129. Alistair Maclean was the Minister at Daviot and Dunlichity, Inverness-shire. He had a wide knowledge of Gaelic folklore and spirituality, which he used not only in his translations from Gaelic into English, but in the English sermons which he preached week by week in his parish Church. One of the hearers of these sermons was his son, also Alistair Maclean, the thriller writer.

69. From *Collected Poems of Joseph Mary Plunkett*, edited by Geraldine Plunkett, 1916. Joseph Mary Plunkett was an Irish aristocrat, with wide ranging interests in scholastic philosophy and mysticism. He was editor of the *Irish Review* and was instrumental in inaugurating the Irish National Theatre.

70. *The Poetical Works of George Macdonald* Chatto & Windus 1911 vol 2 p. 323. See p. 55 *supra*.

71. Adapted for a Christmas Card in 1967: it was headed by '… because there was no place for them in the inn.' *St Luke, Chap. 2 v. 7*; and it began 'If the Child …' instead of 'If love …' Sidney Royse Lysaght was the author of several novels, and of two volumes of verse (*Poems of the Unknown Way*, 1901, and *Horizons and Landmarks*, 1911).

72. Quoted in *George Macleod* Ronald Ferguson, William Collins Sons & Co, Ltd 1990 p. 421. George Fielden Macleod was arguably the most significant minister of the Church of Scotland in the twentieth century. His radical political vision, passionate pacifism, remorseless energy, perception of the material shot through with the spiritual, and his invigorating personality made him a leader not only of the Iona Community which he founded but of many a heart seeking direction and drive in a bewildering world.

73. This poem is included in *Poems for Today: Third Series* published for the English Association by Macmillan and Co., Ltd. 1938 p. 78. Phyllis Hartnoll was the Newdigate Prize-winner at Oxford in 1929, and went on to publish several volumes of poetry.

74. From *The Collected Poems of Ralph Hodgson*. Yorkshire-man Ralph Hodgson worked as a Fleet Street journalist before becoming a lecturer in English Literature at Sendai University, Japan. His interests were not confined to literature: he was also a leading authority on bull terriers.

75. From *Hilaire Belloc The Collected Verse* The Penguin Poets 1958 p. 58. Joseph Hilary Pierre Belloc was a versatile writer of essays, novels, verse, travels, history, biography, and criticism. The fresh, open air blows through his writing: he loved to be out, under the sky, whether tramping over his beloved South Downs; or travelling about France on the new invention, the bicycle; or wandering on foot through the United States, earning his food and lodging at farms by the sketches he made. And all the time – writing his impressions of people and places and recording his views on innumerable subjects. His energy as a writer was prodigious: even when he was a diligent Member of Parliament, books poured from him at the rate of three or four a year, in addition to all the articles he wrote for journals, magazines, and newspapers. His later writings were often devoted to the championing of the best Roman Catholic principles and practices. But it is for his books for children (*The Bad Child's Book of Beasts, Cautionary Tales*) that many people remember him.

76. In *The Church Hymnary: Third Edition* Oxford University Press no. 677. In spite of the fact that he was practically blind by his eighteenth year, George Matheson studied for the ministry of the Church of Scotland, was ordained in 1868 in the parish of Innellan, on the River Clyde, and moved to St Bernard's Parish Church in Edinburgh in 1886. He was a learned scientific theologian and biblical expositor, but it was not until the publication of his *Sacred Songs*, his only volume of verse, that he won a place in the hearts of the Scottish public, principally through this hymn, *O Love, that wilt not let me go.*

77. *The Oxford Book of Prayer* General Editor George Appleton, Oxford University Press 1985 p. 173. *The Christarakana* is the name of the Book of Common Prayer which was in use in the Church of India, Pakistan, Burma, and Ceylon.

78. *Seven Stanzas at Easter* from *Telephone Poles* John Updike, Andre Deutsch Ltd. Updike is known for his novels, such as the Rabbit Angstrom novels, but perhaps not sufficiently known for his poetry.

80. Roy Campbell, from Durban in South Africa, was a man of action as well as a poet. He fought in the Spanish Civil War on the side of Franco, and for the Allies during 1939–45 in North and East Africa. He was an accomplished bull-fighter, and a Talks producer with the BBC.

81. From *The Temple: Sacred Poems and Private Ejaculations* by Mr George Herbert, Facsimile reprint of First Edition, 1633 T Fisher Unwin 1882 p. 150. This book contains nearly all the verse Herbert wrote. His prose works include *A Priest to the Temple*, which contained plain, prudent, practical rules for the country parson, among whose ranks Herbert was proud to number himself, as Rector of Bemerton. At an early period of his university career, he became involved in a now little-

known controversy which brought him into conflict with Scotland's chief presbyterian stalwart, Andrew Melville. Herbert wrote a series of satiric Latin verses in reply to Melville's splendidly named *Anti-Tami-Cami-Categoria* (1604). Melville's work was an attack on the universities of Oxford and Cambridge for passing resolutions hostile to the puritans at the beginning of James 1's reign; Herbert's answer cleverly defended the established Church at all points, and showed him to be strongly opposed to puritanism, an attitude he maintained throughout his life.

82. Psalm 23 in the *Authorised Version* of the *Holy Bible* 1611.

83. From the *Authorised Daily Prayer Book of the United Hebrew Congregations of the British Empire*. Translated by The Reverend S Singer.

85. *Songs of Travel* in *The Complete Poetical Works* vol XX *The Skerryvore Edition* William Heinemann Limited 1924 p. 237. To one of Stevenson's detractors, who had complained that he wrote 'for effect', G K Chesterton retorted by asking, 'But what point is there in writing for anything else?' The delightful effect of his always carefully and skillfully chosen words and rhythms is nowhere more pleasurable than in his *Songs of Travel*, of which this *Bright is the ring of words* is number 15. Ralph Vaughan Williams set the words to music.

86. John Milton grew up familiar with the sounds of the organ. His father was an organist, and doubtless the son often worked the bellows, while his father's
> *volant touch,*
> *Instinct through all proportion low and high,*
> *Fled and pursued transverse the resonant fugue.*

At any rate, the organ-sounds are in all his writings, resonating with mighty harmonies for God and the Truth. His blindness gave him a canvas of utter darkness which he filled with creatures of radiance. To read aloud his *At A Solemn Music* is to rouse and raise the imagination to such a pitch that we catch the music of the choral song of heaven.

87. Wilfred Owen, poet of the First World War, was killed just before the Armistice, and before he was able to complete the book of poetry he had planned, of which he said in the preface 'My subject is War, and the pity of War'. His is one of the authentic and most influential voices of the twentieth century. He spent some time during the war in Craiglockhart Hospital, Edinburgh, where he met Siegfried Sassoon, a fellow-patient.

88. From the opera *Ptolemy*, first performed in 1728 in the King's Theatre, London. By training and inclination Handel was primarily a composer for the theatre, although the popularity of his religious and church music has sometimes masked the extent of his genius. He was a cosmopolitan and eclectic artist, drawing impartially from German, French, Italian, and English traditions. The libretto for *Ptolemy* was written by Nicola Haym, whose method, under close supervision by Handel, was not to exercise his own literary preferences but to adapt older Italian librettos to London taste.

89. Number 16 in R L Stevenson's *Songs of Travel*. See p. 85 *supra*.

90. *Silent Noon* is number 19 in a Sonnet Sequence entitled *The House of Life*. When the full series was published in 1881, there were sixty sonnets in all, arranged in two parts, 'Youth and Change' and 'Change and Fate'. This sonnet has been set to music by Ralph Vaughan Williams. Dante Gabriel Rossetti (full name Gabriel Charles Dante Rossetti), brother of Christina, was known for the first part of his life as an artist and, in 1848, with six other artists he founded the Pre-Raphaelite Brotherhood. But he had also written poetry from an early age, and his poetical works began to rival his paintings for artistry and popularity.

91. William Soutar was born in Perth and lived most of his life in the 'Fair City'. He battled with illness for half a lifetime and he spent his last thirteen years confined to bed. But his spirit was indomitable, and from his battles with disease and death he produced poetry and prose that was potent in lyricism and rich in deep tenderness and dauntless, gusty humour. The main impression his writings leave on the mind is one of joyousness and grace, a testament to the great human virtues of the courage to endure and the courage to create.

92. *The Solitary Reaper* William Wordsworth *The Poetical Works of Wordsworth* Edited by Thomas Hutchison. Revised by Ernest de Selincourt, Oxford University Press 1936 p. 289. Wordsworth made several tours in Scotland, and during the tour of 1803 he began a cordial friendship with Sir Walter Scott . It was on this tour that he saw the solitary reaper, about whom he composed the poem of that name in 1805. See p. 32 *supra*.

93. *The New Oxford Book of English Verse* Chosen and edited by Helen Gardner, Oxford University Press 1972 p. 862. As well as poetry, Siegfried Sassoon wrote semi-autobiographical fiction, and a biography of George Meredith. He enlisted at the beginning of the First World War and was awarded the MC. After the war, he was the editor of the *Daily Herald*. His war poetry is always immediate and vivid, and is frequently caustically trenchant, expressing his bitterness at what he saw as the hypocrisy and romanticism that keep alive the spirit of war.

94. From *The Life of the Spirit and the Life of Today* Evelyn Underhill, Methuen & Co. Ltd, Fourth edition 1923 p. 29. Evelyn Underhill was a woman of large enthusiasms, be it book-binding, yachting, the artistic treasures of France and Italy, wood and metal work, country life and lore, or her love of cats. She began writing before she was sixteen years old, and her first publication, *A Bar-Lamb's Ballad Book* (humorous verses relating to the practice of the law), appeared in 1902. Her kaleido-scopic range of interests served her well when she embraced the Christian faith, and both studied and expounded its principles and practised its precepts. She became notable for conducting Retreats and writing perceptive books on philosophy, religion, and mysticism. She was for some years the theological editor for *The Spectator*, and later for *Time and Tide*. She became a Fellow of King's College, London, and received an honorary degree of DD from Aberdeen University. She made the higher reaches of Christian devotion accessible to a wide range of readers and students, perhaps not least on account of her having a great hatred, as she said, of 'pushing souls about'.

95. *Collins Albatross Book of Verse* Edited by Louis Untermeyer 1960 p.479.
Arthur William Edgar O'Shaughnessy began his adult life as a junior assistant in the
library of the British Museum, and was promoted to an assistantship in the
zoological department. Devoted though he became to science, his real love was
poetry and general literature. The melody of his lyrical verse and his facility in
gorgeous word-painting commanded attention.

97. From the prologue of William Blake's *For the Sexes: The Gates of Parardise.*
Blake, it seems, never went to school. He was the son of a hosier and he trained as
an engraver. His *Songs of Innocence*, which he engraved and published in 1789, gave
early indication of the mystical cast of his mind. Later, he developed a mythology
of his own which makes some of his work difficult to understand. And yet he is
often sublimely simple, relating the all-pervading divine love and sympathy to
trouble and sorrow.

99. From the *Complete Poetry and Selected Prose of John Donne* edited by John Hayward
The Nonesuch Press 1930 p. 321. In the early part of his life, John Donne, the son
of a London ironmonger, was a Roman Catholic. He took Anglican orders in 1615
and preached sermons which are reckoned among the best of the seventeenth
century. He became Dean of St Paul's in 1621, and often preached before Charles I.
His name is usually pronounced and was frequently spelled 'Dunne'.

100. From *Sermons (NT) 13, 2 in Prayers of St Augustine* Barry Ulanov Seabury Press,
Minneapolis, Minnesota, 1983 p. 99.

101. From *The Rule of Columcille.* Quoted in *Scotland: An Anthology* Douglas Dunn,
HarperCollins 1991 p. 173. The *Rule* is first found in Irish in a manuscript in the
Burgundian Library in Brussels. It cannot be traced back beyond the ninth century:
it is unlikely that it was the work of St Columba himself. It does, however, breathe
the spirit of the man, Columba or Columcille ('dove of the Church') of Iona, who
is one of the greatest figures of the early history of Ireland and Scotland. He was
the son of an Ulster chief, and, as a young man, was often embroiled in political
and military affairs. But he turned to more peaceful ways, becoming a recluse at
Glasnevin, and building churches at Derry and other places. He arrived in Scotland
in 563, founded the monastery of Iona, and travelled throughout the mainland
preaching to the Picts. He was a man of complex character, fierce yet compas-
sionate, demonstrating in his own turbulent experience the power of the gospel of
Christ to bring healing and life into a violent and disordered world. The 'red
martyrdom' of the *Rule* means laying down one's life for the faith, while the 'white
martyrdom' involved dying to self and to all attachments, leaving home and family
and embracing perpetual exile. St Columba's Day is 9 June.

102. From *Footprints of the Northern Saints* Darton, Longman & Todd 1996 pp. 75–78
passim. (George) Basil Hume, OSB, Cardinal Archbishop of Westminster and a
monk of Ampleforth Abbey was greatly loved, and is greatly missed, both within
and far beyond the Roman Catholic community in England and Wales. He was a
self-confessed enthusiast for the north-east of England, especially for Northumbria,
whose saints inspired him in every area of his private and public life. He himself

was the outstanding example in Britain in the twentieth century of what he called 'a powerful witness to the primacy of the spiritual in our lives'.

103. From *A Dialogue of Self and Soul*. W B Yeats trained as an artist (both his father and his brother were painters), but he gave up that profession in favour of literature. His publications include volumes of his own poetry, anthologies of verse which he edited, collections of essays, and splendid letters (collected in five notable volumes). He was awarded the Nobel Prize for Literature in 1923. He had an enduring interest in politics, served as a senator of the Irish Free State from 1922 to 1928, and as Chairman of the Commission on Coinage.

104. From Poems by *Coventry Patmore* George Bell and Sons, London 1906 p. 287 (number 10 in a series of Odes under the general title The *Unknown Eros*). Coventry Patmore was an assistant in the printed book department of the British Museum, a friend of Tennyson and Ruskin, and a member of the pre-Raphaelite circle.

105. From *The Temple: Sacred Poems and Private Ejaculations* by Mr George Herbert. Facsimile reprint of First Edition, 1633 T Fisher Unwin 1882 p. 183. See p. 81 *supra*.

106. Quoted in *God of a Hundred Names* Barbara Greene and Victor Gollancz, Victor Gollancz 1962 p. 44. Appollonius was a noted theologian in his day, combatting heresy whenever he encountered it, hence his name, Appollonius the Apologist. He is thought to have been a converted senator of Rome. He was tried for professing Christianity, refused to recant, and was beheaded. This prayer is said to have been adapted from his defence at his 'trial'.

107. From *Oenone* in *The Poetical Works of Alfred, Lord Tennyson* with Introduction and Notes by Arthur Waugh, Collins, London and Glasgow 1904 p. 78. *Oenone* tells the story of the nymph Oenone of Mt Ida, who fell in love with the young shepherd, Paris. After a time of happiness with her, he abandoned her. When he had received his fatal wound, however, he returned to her, seeking her help to cure him. She refused: but later, hearing of his death, took her own life. Lord Tennyson, born and brought up in an Anglican Rectory, won his spurs as a poet when, at Trinity College, Cambridge, he received the Chancellor's medal for English verse in 1829, with a poem entitled *Timbuctoo*. His *In Memoriam*, expressing his grief for his lost friend Arthur Henry Hallam who died in 1833, still resonates in the public mind. In recognition of his work, he received a pension from the Government of £200 per annum. He was appointed Poet Laureate in succession to William Wordsworth in 1850.

108. From the second part of *Pilgrim's Progress*, which was published, together with the first part, in 1684. Bunyan was the son of a tinsmith, and after an elementary education in the village school (Elstow, near Bedford), he began to follow his father's trade. When he was sixteen years old, he was drafted into the Parliamentary army in the Civil War, an experience of soldiering which stood him in good stead when he came to write his *Holy War*. All his writings support his own claim that he 'was never out of the Bible either by reading or meditation'. He preached regularly in a Non-conformist church in Bedford until he was arrested for not having a

licence to preach. He was sent to prison where he spent the next twelve years, during which period he wrote nine of his books. On his release in 1672, he was appointed pastor of the same church in Bedford, but was again imprisoned for a short period, which gave him the opportunity to write the first part of *The Pilgrim's Progress from this World to that which is to come.* On his release he returned to his pastoral charge and continued to preach, but he was never imprisoned again.

109. *Immanence* by Evelyn Underhill in *Poems of Today: Second Series* Sidgwick & Jackson, Ltd. 1922 p. 159. See p. 94 *supra.*

111. From *Prometheus Unbound* This lyrical drama in four acts deals largely with the trials of Prometheus, chained to his rock and subjected to perpetual torture. But it also describes his release by Hercules, and sings of the reign of love that follows when man remains , 'free, uncircumscribed ... Equal, nationless ... the king Over himself; just, gentle, wise, but man.' Shelley drowned while sailing near Spezia, leaving behind him an uncompleted poem, *The Triumph of Life.*

112. Reinhold Niebuhr, theologian, composed this prayer in 1943 and used it as the epigraph for *Justice and Mercy* edited Ursula Niebuhr, Harper & Row 1974. The prayer is used widely, particularly in the Alcoholics Anonymous movement.

113. St Gregory of Sinai. Quoted by St Nilus Sorsky in *A Treasury of Russian Spirituality* edited by G P Fedotor Sheed and Ward.

115. Extract from *Two Quiet Lives* Reader's Union, Constable 1949 pp. 17, 18, 19. Lord (Edward Christian) David (Gascoyne) Cecil was the second son of the fourth Marquess of Salisbury. He followed literature as a career, being a Fellow of both Wadham College and New College, Oxford, before becoming Goldsmiths' Professor of English Literature, Oxford. As well as *Two Quiet Lives*, his books include *Early Victorian Novelists, The Young Melbourne, Max* (a biography of Max Beerbohm), and *A Portrait of Jane Austen.*

116. From *The Oxford Book of English Verse 1250–1900* chosen and edited by Arthur Quiller-Couch, Oxford at the Clarendon Press 1900 p. 390. From the perspective of history, the character of Andrew Marvell seems to have been a glorious contradiction. As a young man he wrote poems in praise of gardens and country life. At the time, he was tutor to the daughter of Lord Fairfax, but when he became tutor to Cromwell's ward, William Dutton, and then Milton's assistant in the Latin secretaryship to the Council, he seemed to lose touch with the beauty and quietness he had so eloquently described. Indeed, after the Restoration, he entered Parliament and became a violent politician, attacking ministers and Charles II himself in fierce satires and stirring pamphlets.

117. From *My Own Garden* Alexander Smith in *A Book of Gardens* edited by Alfred H Hyatt, T N Foulis, Edinburgh and London 1910 p. 37. Alexander Smith, poet and essayist, was an Ayrshire lad who at first followed his father's trade as a pattern designer, but gave it up to became Secretary to Edinburgh University. His *City Poems* give, among other things, a vivid description of Glasgow as he knew it in his

boyhood, and his collection of essays, *Dreamthorp*, offer a splendid reflection of Edinburgh in the dark of winter. His *A Summer in Skye* is still one of the most readable and evocative of travel books.

118. In *The Old Manse* Nathaniel Hawthorne in *Garden Memories* T N Foulis Edinburgh and London 1913 p. 111. Nathaniel Hawthorne was descended from one of the original Puritan Fathers, and the influence of the puritan tradition is evident in many of his writings. His first position in public life was as a customs officer in his home town of Salem, Massachusetts, from which he moved to become American Consul in Liverpool. His novels still command a following, not least *The Scarlet Letter* and *Mosses from an Old Manse.*

119 From *The Temple: Sacred Poems and Private Ejaculations* by Mr George Herbert. Facsimile reprint of First Edition, 1633 T Fisher Unwin 1882 p. 160. See p. 81 *supra.*

121. *Hosea 14: 4–7* in the *Authorised Version* of the *Holy Bible* 1611.

122. *The Collected Poems of Hugh MacDiarmid* vol. 1 Carcanet p. 461. Hugh MacDiarmid was the psuedonym Christopher Murray Grieve chose for himself. He was perhaps Scotland's major literary figure of the twentieth century. He lived a somewhat unsettled life. He was born and brought up in Langholm where his father was the postman; taught in Broughton School in Edinburgh as a pupil-teacher; worked as a journalist in Ebbw Vale, Clydebank, Cupar, and Forfar; served as a sergeant in World War I in the Royal Army Medical Corps; lived in Kildermorie in Easter Ross and in St Andrews before going to live in Montrose where he became a town councillor and a Justice of the Peace; went to London to edit the magazine *Vox*; moved to Liverpool as a public relations officer; then on to Thakeham in Surrey, to Edinburgh, and into a sort of self-imposed exile on Whalsey in Shetland, only to return to the mainland in due course, first to Glasgow, then to Strathaven, and finally to a cottage at Brownsbank near Biggar which became his home until his death in 1978. This impermanency of living reflected the constantly changing scenery of the inner landscape of his mind, supporting now the Scottish Nationalist party, now the Communist Party of Great Britain, returning to the Nationalists and then to the Communists, and all the while working for the revival of Scots letters, sometimes in English, sometimes in the literary Scots that he himself devised. His politics never became popular in his lifetime, but as a poet he was recognised by many as standing in the succession of Dunbar and Burns, and acclaimed as a writer and thinker of international standing.

123. From *The Country Parson's Life* in *The Recreations of a Country Parson First Series* AKHB Longmans, Green and Co. 1881 p. 2 Andrew Kennedy Hutchison Boyd was always known by his initials AKHB, the signature he used for his essays which he began writing for *Fraser's Magazine*, and which in the end amounted to many volumes. But his essays were strictly an avocation: his vocation was the Ministry of the Church of Scotland. He was presented by Queen Victoria to the First Charge of St Andrews in 1865, was Moderator of the General Assembly in 1890, and was appointed a Fellow of King's College, London, in 1895. He played a significant part in the liturgical movement in the Church of Scotland in the last quarter of the nineteenth century.

124. From *A Window in Thrums* Hodder and Stoughton 1889 p. 5. J M Barrie
was born in Kirriemuir, the ninth child of a weaver. His attachment to his mother
became almost an obsession which remained with him all his life. He attended
school successively at Glasgow Academy, Forfar Academy, and Dumfries Academy
before matriculating at Edinburgh University, where he studied English under
Professor David Masson. He began his professional life as a journalist, and
continued to write for newspapers and journals while pursuing his more notable
career as a playwright. His plays won him immense popularity, and his Never-Never
Land inhabited by Peter Pan and Wendy became part of the landscape of
childhood. Although he is sometimes dismissed as merely belonging to the
'Kailyard School', his command of language and grasp of stagecraft, together with
his flair for creating realistic characters, make him a dramatist to be reckoned with.
He received a baronetcy in 1913 for his services to literature, and was appointed to
the Order of Merit in 1922, the year in which he was elected Rector of St Andrews
University. He also served as Chancellor of Edinburgh University.

125. *The Quiet Heart* George Appleton Collins (Fount) 1983 p. 42. George Appleton
served the Anglican communion in many parts of the world. He began his ministry
as a curate in East London, and when he retired he was Archbishop of Jerusalem. In
between, he had served as a missionary in the Irrawaddy Delta, Warden of the
Theological College of Holy Cross in Rangoon, Director of Public Relation for the
Burma Government in Exile during the Japanese occupation in the Second World
War and Archdeacon of Rangoon, Secretary of the Conference of British
Missionary Societies, Rector of St Botolph's, Aldgate, in the City of London,
Archdeacon of London and Canon of St Paul's Cathedral, and as Archbishop of
Perth in Western Australia. Remarkable as all this is, it was his devotional writings
that endeared him to a large public in the last quarter of the twentieth century.

126. In *Poems of Christina Rossetti* Chosen and edited by William M Rossetti.
Macmillan & Co 1904 (Golden Treasury Series) p. 290, where it appears under the
title *Sea Sand and Sorrow*. Christina Rossetti's work ranged from poems of fantasy and
verses for children to religious poetry: the latter came to form the greater part of her
writings. She had written poetry from an early age: first, at the age of twelve, verses
to her mother, printed privately by her grandfather; and then, at the age of nineteen,
under the pseudonym Ellen Alleyne, in the journal her brother Dante Gabriel
Rossetti and his friends had established, *The Germ*. The melancholy cast which
sometimes appears in her work has been accounted for by the fact that her rather
excessive devotional Church-life estranged her from her suitor to whom she was
deeply attached. She also suffered as an invalid, and for two years her life hung by a
thread. Although she recovered, she never again enjoyed good health. Her poems are
marked by a degree of technical perfection; in even her slightest lyrics, there is the
touch of genius.

127. *A Child's Garden of Verses* Robert Louis Stevenson. Facsimile edition Mainstream
1990 p. 44. See pp. 8, 64 *supra*.

129. In William Blake's *Several Questions Answered* in *MS Note-Book* p. 99. See p. 97 *supra*.

130. From *The Oxford Book of Scottish Verse* chosen by John MacQueen and Tom Scott, Clarendon Press 1966 p. 549. George Bruce, a poet from Fraserburgh, is inspired by the rugged land and sea-scapes of his native North-east. He has written much that sings of the permanence of the land and the durability of its people, of the agelessness of the sea and man's struggle against it, and of the irresistible tides of history. But his clarity is perhaps nowhere more lambent than when he writes of childhood, which for him is not just a fact and an event in its own right, but a symbol of immutable spiritual realities.

131. XI in *Songs of Travel* in *The Complete Poetical Works vol XX The Skerryvore Edition* p. 237. See p. 85 *supra*.

132. *The Poetical Works of Thomas Hood* Ward, Lock, & Co, Warwick House p. 260. Thomas Hood was born in London, but, when his health failed in his middle teens, he was sent to his father's relations in Dundee to recuperate. He spent some three years in the city and while there, he began writing for local newspapers. On his return to London, he trained as an engraver, but the work was too much for his health and he turned to literature. He became the editor of the *London Magazine*, whose brilliant staff included de Quincey, Lamb, and Hazlitt. His poetry took off in two directions: his humorous verses, for which he is perhaps chiefly remembered, are still a delight (few could, or can, match his facility of playing upon words); and his more serious work, such as the *Bridge of Sighs* and *Song of the Shirt*. He is perhaps at his best when the humourous and the serious are combined, as in his *Miss Kilmansegg*. But his *I remember, I remember* is in all our hearts.

133. In *Thomas and Jane* Ian Campbell, Friends of Edinburgh University Library: Edinburgh 1980 p. 43. Jane Welsh Carlyle wrote nothing for publication, but her letters are a constant source of wonder and pleasure. Her brilliantly independent mind and her winning command of language made good her family's claim that she could trace her descent both to John Knox and William Wallace. After a protracted and confusing courtship, she and Thomas Carlyle were married. They eventually settled in Chelsea.

134. In *Poem for the Day* Edited by Nicholas Albery, Sinclair-Stevenson 1994 p. 266. Lawrence singing hymns is not the usual picture we have of the man who wrote *Lady Chatterley's Lover*. He was born the son of a Nottinghamshire miner whose bullying caused the boy to rely more and more on his mother whom he adored. She encouraged him to escape the mines through education: he attended University College, Nottingham, and became a schoolmaster before adopting writing as his profession. He and his wife Frieda lived mostly abroad, in Italy, Australia, and New Mexico. He died in Vence, near Nice. His works include not only the well-known novels, but short stories, essays, and several volumes of poems.

135. In *The Ring of Words* introduced by Andrew Motion, Sutton Publishing 1998 p. 126. In 1998, more than seven thousand poems were entered for *The Daily Telegraph* Avron International Poetry Competition. *The Ring of Words* comprises the winning entries and the cream of the runners-up: Tony Horwood's poem, *The Lost Island of St Kilda*, is among them.

136. Samuel Taylor Coleridge was born at Ottery St Mary, the tenth son of the family. His father, vicar and master of the grammar school, was a learned and simple man much given to absent-mindedness, who from time to time addressed his congregation in Hebrew. Samuel was a precocious and imaginative child who grew up to be a poet, a critic, and a philosopher. He was a schoolboy friend of Charles Lamb (Christ's Hospital), and later at Cambridge he came to know and admire Southey and Lovell. He was known as a totally incapable horseman, incurably poor, and the town's most entertaining talker – three characteristics which he maintained throughout his life. He made various more or less successful attempts at journalism, but the public generally preferred his poetry and public lectures (on such subjects as political philosophy or the English poets). He met Wordsworth in 1795, and a warm friendship sprang up between them. His use of opium is well known: he may have taken it in the first instance to boost his health which had been undermined when he was a schoolboy. His *Rime of the Ancient Mariner* and *Kubla Khan*, to mention but two of his achievements, with their narrative power and air of brooding mystery, reveal a master at work.

137. *The Complete Poems of Robert Bridges* Oxford University Press. Robert Bridges, the son of a Kentish squire, graduated BA in Wadham College, Oxford before proceeding to the study of medicine at St Bartholomew's Hospital in London. He served for a time (successively) as casualty physician at St Bartholomew's, physician at the Great Northern Hospital, and as a general practitioner. In 1882, he gave up medical practice and settled in Yattendon in Berkshire, devoting himself to literature, in which he had already made his mark as a poet of unusual and distinctive gifts. He was appointed Poet Laureate in 1913. He was a scholar of great learning, and a skilled and cultivated musician. He was perhaps too subtle and technical a poet to appeal to a wide public, but his *Yattendon Hymnal* was a seminal book in the development of hymnody in the twentieth century. He was intimately associated with the Oxford University Press, taking an active and expert interest in such things as typeface, spelling, and music notation. He did much to make printing an art form.

138. In *The Collected Poems of John Masefield* William Heinemann Ltd 1925 p. 64. The sea was in John Masefield's blood and in his poetry too. He ran away to sea in early life, and its rhythms pervade much of his writing. He crossed the Atlantic and travelled around America, working at whatever jobs he could find. All the time he was reading widely in the English poets and trying his hand at his own efforts in verse. On his return to England, he attracted attention with his Salt *Water Ballads* which included *Cargoes*, with its magical sea-going images and rhythms (*Dirty British coaster with a salt-caked smoke stack* …). His touch became even surer, and the poetry began to flow. And not just poetry. He wrote several naval histories, and, sometimes in collaboration with his wife, edited selections of the works of various poets and dramatists. He was also a novelist, a playwright, and a critic. He had a perennially youthful spirit, and there are few more enchanting children's books than his *The Box of Delights*. He was appointed Poet Laureate in 1930, and received the Order of Merit in 1935.

139. In *The Best Loved Poems of the American People* edited Hazel Felleman. Karle Wilson Baker was born in Little Rock, Arkansas, but she spent most of her adult life in Nacogdoches in Texas, where she married a local banker, raised two children, and taught in several universities. All the time she was writing: personal and historical essays, novels, nature poetry, and short stories. In 1931, the third volume of her poems, *Dreamers on Horseback*, was nominated for the Pulitzer Prize for poetry.

140. *The Desk Drawer Anthology* compiled and selected by Alice Roosevelt Longworth and Theodore Roosevelt, Hutchinson & Co, London p. 130. Frederick William Farrar – Dean Farrar, as he is always known – began his public life as a teacher, first in Harrow and then at Marlborough. When he wrote *I am only one* he was a Canon of Westminster and Rector of St Margaret's Parish Church. Crowds flocked to hear his powerful preaching, and he used his popularity as a lever to restore the ancient St Margaret's (he spent £30,000 on it, completely re-ordering its interior) and to re-establish it as the parish Church of the Palace of Westminster. He became Chaplain to the Speaker of the House of Commons. Later, when he was appointed Dean of Canterbury, he threw himself into the restoration of the Cathedral. He is remembered for his story *Eric: or Little by Little* and for his *Life of Christ*, though few nowadays read either book: the title is perhaps the best part of the first; and the honest and robust faith matched by wide and accurate scholarship were not quite enough to save the second from Farrar's florid style.

141. *Courtesy in Hilaire Belloc Collected Verse* in *The Penguin Poets* with an Introduction by Ronald Knox Penguin press 1958 p. 57. See p. 75 *supra*.

143. *Song of Songs 8: 6, 7* in the *Authorised Version* of the *Holy Bible* 1611.

145. In *The Oxford Book of English Verse 1250–1900* chosen & edited by Arthur Quiller-Couch, Oxford at the Clarendon Press 1900 p. 683. James Henry Leigh Hunt, essayist, critic, and poet, will always be remembered for his *Abou Ben Adhem* and *Jenny Kissed Me*. But he wrote far more prose than poetry, and is especially significant in the development of the light essay. Some of his writings landed him in trouble with the authorities. He and his brother were each fined £500 and imprisoned for two years for an outspoken article against the Prince Regent which appeared in the *Examiner*, the magazine they edited. Though in his usual delicate health, Hunt refused to be cowed: in a splendid display of his characteristically indomitable and cheerful spirit, he continued to edit *The Examiner* from jail, papered the walls of his (admittedly roomy) cell with a trellis of roses, painted the ceiling with sky and clouds, furnished the windows with Venetian blinds, and arranged for an unfailing supply of flowers. He surrounded himself with books and busts, and installed his pianoforte. He was constantly visited by such people as Byron, Moore, Bentham, and Lamb, and was able to continue not only his journalism but also his essay writing and criticism. He was one of the first to recognise the genius of Shelley and Keats, and introduced them in the pages of *The Examiner* to the public. He received a civil list pension in 1847.

146. In *Poems of Christina Rossetti* chosen and edited by William M Rossetti Macmillan & Co 1904 (Golden Treasury Series) p. 280. The poem is called *The Birthday*. See p. 125 *supra*.

147. In *The Oxford Book of Scottish Verse* chosen by Tom MacQueen and Tom Scott, Clarendon Press 1966 p. 100. Little is known of Dunbar's life, but it is probable he was born in East Lothian and was a student at St Andrew's University. His name appears on the Privy Seal record in 1500 as being paid an annual pension of ú10 as court poet. His pension was increased to £20 in 1507, and £80 in 1510. He was perhaps the most notable of Scotland's mediaeval 'makars', creatively and comprehensively ranging over a wide variety of subjects. His exuberant and penetrating satires expose the evils of contemporary Church, court, and town life; his poems on personal matters reveal his occasional despondency and despair (he suffered from migraine: see his poem *On his heid-ake*); his courtly love poems are gems in that tradition; and his religious poems demonstrate both his linguistic virtuosity and his spiritual perception.

148. In *The Oxford Book of Scottish Verse* chosen by Tom MacQueen and Tom Scott, Clarendon Press 1966 p. 406. Whatever else may be said of Robert Burns, he was a worker, both as a farmer on his successive farms where his back-breaking toil on poor soil scarcely made him a living, and as a poet and songwriter, producing a vast output of material. Although he is loved all the world over, he is not understood everywhere. How could one man be so tender and rough, so delicate and coarse, so spiritual and sensual, so soaring and earthy, all at the same time? The truth is that he looked at life from more than one angle, and was able to hold its many contradictions in tension, even if not always in balance. His poems and songs are full not only of the history and traditions of Scotland, but of his own convoluted and often contradictory experience. The songs are his masterpieces, melding poetry and music into an indissoluble and wonderful union. His love songs still captivate the world. He remains Scotland's national bard, and in Scotland and beyond is celebrated with affection, pride, and gratitude each year on Burns's Nicht, 25 January, the anniversary of his birth.

149. In *The New Oxford Book of English Verse 1250–1950* chosen and edited by Helen Gardner, Oxford University Press 1972 p. 308. James Graham, 'the great Marquis', is one of Scotland's heroes. In the turbulent seventeenth century, he towers above others as a man of principle and courage, true to the cause he embraced, and true to himself. He was an early supporter of the National Covenant, but he declined to follow the policies of his fellow Covenanter, the Earl of Argyll, and was imprisoned in Edinburgh Castle. In the Civil War, he proved himself to be a brilliant general, leading the army of King Charles I. But he was finally defeated at Philiphaugh, and fled to the continent where he spent five years trying to raise support for the Royalist Cause. On his return to Scotland, he was defeated at a skirmish in Carbisdale, near Ardgay. He retreated into Assynt, but was betrayed by Munro of Lemlair and brought to Edinburgh where he was executed in 1650.

150. *The Collected Letters of Thomas and Jane Welsh Carlyle* Duke-Edinburgh Edition Volume iv (Durham, N C 1970) p. 42. See pp. 26 and 133 *supra*.

151. *Sonnets from the Portuguese* number 43. Elizabeth Barret married Robert Browning in 1846, and 'The Barrets of Wimpole Street' have been in the public eye ever since. Elizabeth must have been an engaging child: she had an amazing gift for learning, and at the age of eight could read Homer in the original, holding her book in one hand and nursing her doll with the other. When she was thirteen, her epic *Battle of Marathon* was written in four books, and her father had it printed. She grew up to be 'the princess of poets' (George Macdonald) and, though small and pale, was a strikingly beautiful woman. The quality of her poetry was such that there was a move to have her appointed as Poet Laureate in succession to Wordsworth. After her marriage, she spent most of her life in Italy, where she died.

152. Robert Burns. In *The Oxford Book of Scottish Verse* chosen by Tom MacQueen and Tom Scott, Clarendon Press 1966 p. 494. See p. 145 *supra*.

153. From *Maud* in *The Poetical Works of Alfred, Lord Tennyson* with Introduction and Notes by Arthur Waugh section XXII, stanzas i, ii, iii, vi, vii, and viii Collins, London and Glasgow 1904 p. 505. See p. 107 *supra*.

155. In *A Shropshire Lad* in *The Collected Poems of A E Houseman* Jonathan Cape 1939 p. 35. A E Houseman was the eldest child of Edward Houseman, a solicitor. He had four brothers and two sisters. He was educated at Bromsgrove School where he won a scholarship to St John's College, Oxford. He entered the Civil Service as a clerk in the Patent Office, but continued to study the classics in which he had excelled while at College. He became an outstanding classicist, holding first the Chair of Latin in University College, London, before moving to the Chair of Latin at Cambridge where he was elected to a fellowship in Trinity College. He published three volumes of poetry, notable for their clarity and simplicity. It was said of his poetry that 'every poem has phrases that no one else could have written'.

157. From *The Heart of Midlothian* chapter 40 Sir Walter Scott, Bart Thomas Nelson 1901 p. 524 (*Proud Maisie* was sung by Madge Wildfire as she lay dying). Nobody could tell a story better than Scott. His great ballad-epics are simply romantic stories set against the backcloth of Scottish history, and his novels are a stage where his characters play out their vivid lives of tragedy or comedy. His novels were published anonymously, perhaps because he loved mystery, was a little sensitive to criticism, and felt that writing novels was not quite a fitting occupation for a man in his position: he was, after all, a Writer to the Signet, Sheriff-Depute of Selkirkshire, and Clerk of the Court of Session. His historical and antiquarian writings make a fair claim for him to be treated as a historian, and his critical works are learned and perceptive. He was a great defender of the rights of Scotland, and his three letters *From Malachi Malagrowther* and his *Thoughts on the Proposed Change of Currency* are not entirely irrelevant to the present debate on a European single currency! The essence of the man lay not only in his patriotism, but in his personal moral courage. When he was drawn into the financial crash of his printer and publisher, Ballantyne and Constable, and their English agents, Hurst Robinson and Company, he too was declared bankrupt. He vowed to pay his debts through writing – 'This right hand shall work it all off,' he told Lord Cockburn – and the debt was fully repaid shortly before his death.

158. In *Poems of Christina Rossetti* Macmillan & Co 1904 (Golden Treasury Series) p. 269. See p. 126 *supra.*

159. Robert Burns. In *The New Oxford Book of English Verse* chosen and edited by Helen Gardner, Oxford University Press 1972 p. 491. See p. 145 *supra.*

160. From *Light in Among the Flowers* 1878. Bourdillon spent most of his life tutoring private pupils and preparing them for university. As well as writing poetry, he made several translations from the high Romance literature of France.

161. Elizabeth Barrett Browning. See p. 148 *supra.*

162. Anonymous, early 16th century.

163. From *Numbers 14: 21* in the *Authorised Version* of the *Holy Bible* 1611.

165. *To be a Pilgrim* Basil Hume, St Paul Publications SPCK 1984 p. 169 See p. 102 *supra.*

166. *Collected Poems of Oliver St John Gogarty* Constable 1952. Oliver St John Gogarty came from a line of physicians, and was himself a successful specialist nose and throat surgeon. He was a colourful character, often distracted from his medical work by literary pursuits, bicycle-racing (he was of championship class), politics, aviation (he was the pioneer aviator of Dublin) and conviviality. He was a Senator in the first Senate of the Irish Free State and took a prominent part in the early days of the Republic. He had a genius for friendship, drawing within his circle such men as James Joyce, W B Yeats, and Augustus John. The vigour and spontaneity of his mind, matched by a robust and scintillating flair for language, gained him a reputation as a wit and a welcome into congenial literary and artistic circles. In spite of a tendency to showmanship (his fur coat and yellow Rolls-Royce were recognised everywhere), he produced several novels, volumes of reminiscences, and books of poetry.

167. *Auguries of Innocence* William Blake Lines 1–4 See p. 97 *supra.*

168. Adapted from *The Conversations and Exhortation of Father Zossima* in *The Brothers Karamazov.* Quoted in *God of a Hundred Names* Barbara Greene and Victor Gollancz, Victor Gollancz 1962 p. 95. Dostoevsky was a deeply religious man with his own mystical ideas of Russian Orthodox Christianity. He had an abhorrence of rationalism and socialism. His novels are notable for their penetrating insight into psychologically disturbed characters, and for their exploration of the humour of the absurd.

169. *Centuries of Meditation* Quoted in *The Oxford Book of English Prose* chosen and edited by Sir Arthur Quiller-Couch Oxford University Press 1827 p. 308. Thomas Traherne wrote religious works, in both prose and verse. His writings are marked by originality of thought and musicality of expression.

170. In the *Scottish Psalter* 1929 Oxford University Press Number 148(2). This version of Psalm 148, which appeared in the *Scottish Psalter* of 1650, was one of the few psalms in that psalter not in short metre, common metre, or long metre. It is popular in Scotland to this day. George Wither had led a colourful life as a young man, being imprisoned on more than one occasion. He was an accomplished poet, with satires, pastorals, eclogues and love poems to his name. In the 1620's he became a convinced Puritan, and thereafter wrote religious exercises, notably his *Hymnes and Songs of the Church*, of which this psalm is one.

172. *The Poetical Works of Wordsworth* edited by Thomas Hutchison, Revised by Ernest de Selincourt Oxford University Press 1936 p. 79. This poem is included among those which refer to Wordworth's childhood. See p. 32 *supra*.

173. *Poems by Coventry Patmore* p. 428. See p. 104 *supra*.

174. *The Collected Poems of Katherine Tynan* Macmillan and Company This poem is also found in *Collins Albatross Book of Verse* William Collins, Sons and Company 1960 p. 503. Katherine Tynan was the daughter of a farmer in a spectacularly beautiful part of Ireland (Whitehall, Clondalkin, co. Dublin). She was a clever child, and with her dog, her sugar stick, and her book under her arm, 'she learned all the mysteries of the fields.' She wrote more than a hundred novels by which she made a pleasant living, and at intervals she published collections of poems. She was in touch with the leaders of the Irish literary movement, including W B Yeats and George Russell. She married a barrister, Henry Albert Hinkson, by whom she had two sons.

175. In *Poems of Christina Rossetti* chosen and edited by William M Rossetti Macmillan & Co 1904 (Golden Treasury Series) p. 217. See p. 125 supra.

176. In *A Shropshire Lad* in *The Collected Poems of A E Houseman* Jonathan Cape 1939 p. 11 See p. 152 *supra*.

177. Emily Dickinson was an American poet who lived almost as a recluse in Amherst, Massachusetts, where she was born. Privacy and solitude were important to her: none of her poems was published during her life, with the exception of two which appeared without her permission. She left over a thousand poems in manuscript, which were published by Thomas H Johnston in 1955. Her work, lyrical, mystical, and practical (often dealing with domestic realities), and full of wit, shows her to stand in the first rank of poets.

178. Anonymous

179. In *A Little Book of Modern Verse*, with an Introduction by T S Eliot selected by Anne Ridler, Faber and Faber 1941 p. 34. T E Hulme was killed in action in the First World War. In addition to his own poems, he published translations of Bergsen and George Sorel.

180. *The Poetry of Robert Frost* edited by Edward Connery Lathem, Jonathan Cape Ltd. Robert Frost is one of the most popular of modern American poets. He was born in San Francisco, of New England stock, and moved to New England in his early life. He farmed for about three years in England, and on his return to New England, he supported himself by teaching in a succession of colleges. Ten volumes of his poetry have been published, the last one in 1962.

181. *The Collected Poems of Thomas Hardy*. Thomas Hardy was pronounced stillborn by the surgeon who attended his mother, but the midwife roused the life in him. He was born into a family in Higher Bockhampton, near Stinsford in Dorset, which had a passion for music. They made Stinsford Parish Church celebrated for the instrumental music they played at the services; they were always ready to play at secular festivities as well. Hardy's father was also an expert country dancer, and was profoundly attached to the manners and customs of rural life as well as to the wild nature of the country-side: he liked to lie on a bank in hot weather 'with the grasshoppers leaping over him'. Hardy himself often played the fiddle at local dance parties. Much of this buoyant rural atmosphere is reflected in Hardy's novels and poems where he paints glorious pictures of country life and character, at the same time as dealing with the ironies and disappointments of life and love and recounting the struggle of man against the force that rules the world. He received the Order of Merit in 1910. He died in 1928: his body was buried in Westminster Abbey, but his heart was buried in the churchyard of Stinsford.

182. In *Collins Albatross Book of Verse* William Collins, Sons and Company 1960 p. 459. Thomas Edward Brown was born in, and remained devoted to, the Isle of Man. The greater part of his poems are published in the Manx dialect and deal with themes dear to the hearts of the islanders who are very warm admirers of his work. He was a Fellow of Oriel College, Oxford, and second master at Clifton.

183. From *Collected Poems of William Soutar* Andrew Dakers 1948. See p. 91 *supra*.

184. *The Collected Poems of G K Chesterton* Cecil Palmer 1927 p. 297. Gilbert Keith Chesterton's mother, Marie Louise Grosjean, was of French and Scottish blood: the 'Keith' in his name comes from her maternal ancestors, the Keiths of Aberdeen. His father's administrative skills as an auctioneer and estate agent were not inherited by his son who, even as a schoolboy, displayed the characteristics for which he was notorious: he was absent-minded and good-natured almost to a fault. He was also, even at that age, remarkable for the rock-like strength with which he held and maintained his point of view, expressing it in word or drawing it with stunning originality and flair. He grew up to be a man of such industry and insight that philosophers, poets, men of letters, historians, journalists, detective story readers, and radio listeners – each and all could recognize him as more than capable in *their* field and even sometimes brilliant. And all the time he was engaged in a voyage of discovery, which brought him home to harbour only in 1922 when he was received into the Roman Catholic Church. The questing spirit, delightful, childlike, wondering, was his until the end.

185. *Sheep Tracks* by M H Noël Paton first appeared in *A Wanderer's Lute* Alexander Moring, Ltd, London, but for this book is taken from *A Hebridean Medley*, which was privately printed by Macrae & Patterson, 96 Nicolson Street, Edinburgh.

186. *Collected Poems of Kathleen Raine* Hamish Hamilton.

187. In *The Nation's Favourite Poems* Foreword by Griff Rhys Jones, BBC Books 1996 p. 108. Walter de la Mare was educated at St Paul's Cathedral Choristers' School where he edited the school magazine. For a time after leaving school, he worked for the Anglo-American Oil Company, but his first love was writing, and he published his first book, *Songs of Childhood*, in 1902. He wrote vastly, as a poet, novelist, and anthologist, perhaps more successfully for children than for adults. He lived in a sort of fantasy world, where everything was the mirror-image of itself: his first book was published under the name Walter Ramal, an adaption of de la Mare read in a mirror. His poetry is full of involuntary and sometimes astonishing inversions, as though he were always turning to the mirror to look out on life in reflection. He used to say that the moonlight (another reflection) was the chief illuminant of his field of vision (as in the poem here, Silver). He knew the craft of the poet, however, and guarded his flock of unruly words with jealousy and care. He received honorary degrees from the universities of Oxford, Cambridge, London, St Andrews, and Bristol. He was appointed Companion of Honour in 1948, and awarded the Order of Merit in 1953.

188. The original title of this poem is *I am the Great Sun (from a Normandy crucifix of 1632)*. It appears in *Modern Religious Poetry*, p. 9. Charles Causley was born at Launceston in Cornwall. He is a writer, poet, editor, and teacher. During the Second World War, he served in the Royal Navy. His works are increasingly finding their way into anthologies of popular verse.

189. *Intimations of Immortality from Recollections of Early Childhood* stanzas I and II William Wordsworth in *The Poetical Works of Wordsworth* edited by Thomas Hutchison. Revised by Ernest de Selincourt Oxford University Press 1936 p. 587. See p. 32 *supra*.

191. *St Mark 14: 36* in the *Authorised Version* of the *Holy Bible* 1611

193. Edith Barfoot. Quoted in *The Quiet Heart* George Appleton Collins (Fount) 1983 p. 386

194. *The New Oxford Book of English Verse* chosen and edited by Helen Gardner Oxford University Press 1972 p. 918. *From Musée des Beaux Arts*. W H Auden was born in York where his father was a medical practitioner and a classicist and his mother was a nurse and a high Anglican. At his preparatory school, Hindhead in Surrey, he met Christopher Isherwood, and they became life-long friends. At Christ Church, Oxford he established himself as a leader of the young poets of his generation. He lived for a time in Berlin under the Weimar Republic where he encountered at first hand the emerging threat of Nazi dominance; and during the Spanish Civil War he served on the Republican side as a stretcher-bearer. For a time,

he took up school-mastering, including a spell at Larchfield Academy in Helensburgh. He was known as Uncle Wiz to his pupils, one of whom described his teaching as a non-stop firework display. He left Britain for America, taking out citizenship there but not losing his contact with or his love for Europe. He was Professor of Poetry at Oxford from 1956 to 1961. In his young years he had been influenced by Marxist ideas, but later he took the Christian faith seriously, practising it in the simplest way, with kindness to everyone, forgiveness for those who had wronged him, and love as the centre and the strength of everyday living. The unique stamp of his poetry was matched by the unique stamp of his appearance and personality, with his crumpled suit, his carpet slippers, and his wonderfully craggy face which became in age like a crinkled parchment.

195. Anonymous

196. *Poem for The Day* edited by Nicholas Albery, Sinclair-Stevenson 1994 p. 278.
Mary Coleridge's grandfather was the nephew of Samuel Taylor Coleridge. She was a novelist as well as a poet, but, although Robert Louis Stevenson praised her novel, *The Seven Sleepers of Ephesus*, she received little notice during her lifetime. Volumes of her poems were published posthumously, and some of them are now highly regarded.

197. *Poem for The Day* edited by Nicholas Albery, Sinclair-Stevenson 1994 p. 334.
Thomas Hardy considered Charlotte Mew to be the best woman poet of her day. She developed a talent for writing verse and prose early in her life, and from the age of twenty was a regular contributor to *Temple Bar*. The best of her poems may be found in *The Farmer's Bride* (1915) and *The Rambling Sailor* (1929).

198. *Intimations of Immortality* from *Recollections of Early Childhood* stanza V
William Wordsworth in *The Poetical Works of Wordsworth* edited by Thomas Hutchison, Revised by Ernest de Selincourt Oxford University Press 1936 p. 587.
See p. 32 *supra*.

199. *Triad* by William Sharp, in *The Oxford Book of Mystical Verse* chosen by D H S Nicholson and A H E Lee, 1917 Oxford University Press p. 400. See p. 37 *supra*.

200. *To the Immortal Memory ... of ... Sir Lucius Carey and Sir H Morison* 1640.
'O rare Ben Jonson', as he was called on the tombstone of one of his contemporaries, has become his own epitaph, on account both of his effervescent personality and multi-faceted gifts. He was a bricklayer, soldier, actor, playwright, and poet. He came to Scotland to visit Drummond of Hawthornden.

201. Hugh MacDiarmid in *The Oxford Book of Scottish Verse* Tom MacQueen and Tom Scott Clarendon Press 1966 p. 487. See p. 122 *supra*.

202. *Ecclesiastical History of the English People* book ii, chapter 13 translated by B. Colgrave 1969 *Oxford Dictionary of Quotations Fourth Edition* edited by Angela Partington 1992 p. 58. Bede grew up under the guidance of Benedict Biscop, abbot of Wearmouth, then went to the monastery at Jarrow where he spent the greater

part of his life as a scholarly monk and historian. He was buried at Jarrow, but his bones were taken to Durham during the first half of the eleventh century. The title 'Venerable' was first added to his name in the century following his death.

203. From *The New Oxford Book of English Verse 1250–1950* chosen and edited by Helen Gardner 1972 p. 113. It was Sir Walter Scott who told the story (in *Kenilworth*) of Sir Walter Raleigh laying down his cloak in a muddy spot at Greenwich for Queen Elizabeth to step on. True or not, the story catches the spirit of the man, courtly, courageous, self-possessed. His life oscillated between the adventure of voyages of discovery to the American continent and expeditions to the Orinoco in search of gold, and imprisonment in the Tower of London. On two different occasions he was unjustly sentenced to death. He was executed at Westminster where his remains were buried in St Margaret's Church. He wrote both prose and verse, but much of his poetry is lost, with only some thirty short pieces surviving. [Note: *The Oxford Book of English Verse* edited by Christopher Rick Oxford University Press 1999 p. 66 assigns this poem to 'Anonymous', and asserts 'formerly attributed to Sir Walter Raleigh'.]

205. George Fox in *God of a Hundred Names* Barbara Greene and Victor Gollancz, Victor Gollancz 1962 p. 19. See p. 1 *supra*.

207. *The Cry of the Deer*

208. *The Cry of the Deer*

209. Source unknown

210. Source unknown. At the age of fourteen, Theresa was sent to a convent by her father for flirting, and, to her surprise, found that she could take to the discipline there. She took the veil at a Carmelite house in Avila at the age of eighteen, and for the rest of her life devoted herself to prayer. She became known for her remarkable visions, which even at the time were recognised as signs of her rare and powerful sanctity. Although dogged with ill-health, she founded several houses herself, both for nuns and for friars. She was canonised in 1621.

211. Quoted in *To be a Pilgrim* Basil Hume OSB, St Paul Publications SPCK 1984 p. 178. These were the last words spoken by The Queen in a speech at the dinner in the Guild Hall in London on the evening of the official celebrations of the Jubilee of Her Majesty's reign.

212. Leigh Hunt. *A Book of English Poetry: Chaucer to Rossetti* collected and edited by G B Harrison Pelican Books 1937 p. 170. See p. 143 *supra*.

213. Edwin Markham *Collins Albatross Book of Verse* edited by Louis Untermeyer Collins 1960 p. 487.

214. W B Yeats. *He Wishes for the Cloths of Heaven* See p. 103 *supra*.

215. *Psalm 31: 6* in the *Authorised Version* of the *Holy Bible* 1611.

217. John Greenleaf Whittier in *Church Hymnary: Revised Edition* Oxford University Press 1927 number 558 See p. 36 *supra*.

218. Forms of this poem in French go back to the fifteenth century. This version is found on the title-page of a Book of Hours, *Pynson's Horae*, 1514. It was first printed as a hymn in *The Oxford Hymn Book*, 1908. The tune, by Walford Davies, first appeared as a leaflet in 1910.

219. Quoted in *The Quiet Heart* George Appleton Collins (Fount) 1983 p. 464. William of Thierry was a mystic of the early twelfth century.

220. Leo Marks. The only information to hand about this poem is that it may be entitled *Code Poem for the French Resistance*.

221. Thomas Hardy. Set to music by Barbara Rawling See p. *179 supra*.

222. *The New Oxford Book of English Verse 1250–1950* chosen and edited by Helen Gardner Oxford University Press 1972 p. 629. Thomas Lovell Beddoes was a medical practitioner by profession, but his real love was writing. His works show that he had a taste for the macabre and supernatural, but his poignant lyrics are haunting in their beauty. *This Dream Pedlary* has been set to music by John Ireland.

223. *The Oxford Dictionary of Quotations Fourth Edition* edited by Angela Partington Oxford University Press 1992 p. 256. The long title of this short poem, *Vitae Summa Brevis Spem Nos Vetat Incohare Longham*, is a line from Horace's Odes, book 1, no. 4, line 15, and it means 'Life's short span forbids us to enter on far-reaching hopes'. Ernest Dowson's book of poems consists largely of translations from Latin, the best known one of which is *I have been faithful to thee, Cynara! in my fashion*.

224. John Greenleaf Whittier in *Church Hymnary: Revised Edition* Oxford University Press 1927 number 589. See p. 36 *supra*.

225. *The Collected Poems of Stevie Smith* 1975. Stevie Smith (Florence Margaret Smith) was born in Hull, but moved to London at the age of three, where she was brought up by her mother, and her aunt whom she immortalized in *Novel on Yellow Paper* as 'lion aunt'. Her talent flourished in her novels, but her creative genius perfected itself in her poetry, always sharp in vivid imagery, free-running, and with strong rhymes. Her wittiest lines often point to deep, if sometimes grim, truths.

226. *This England* magazine. John Gillespie Magee was born in Shanghai, the son of Episcopalian missionaries to China. His father was American and his mother British. During the Battle of Britain, he enlisted in the Royal Canadian Air Force, became a Spitfire pilot, and first saw action north of Dunkirk, on 8 November 1941. On 11 December he was killed in a mid-air collision with another British plane, whose pilot was also killed. Pilot Officer Magee was nineteen years old when he died. Four months earlier he wrote *High Flight*, which has the sub-title *An Airman's Ecstasy*.

Following the *Challenger* Space Shuttle disaster in 1986, President Reagan quoted from this poem in his tribute to the men who died.

227. *The Poetical Works of Alfred, Lord Tennyson* Macmillan and Co. Limited, The Globe Edition 1899 p. 636 . See p. 107 *supra*.

228. *The Complete Poems of Emily Jane Brontë* edited by C W Hatfield Oxford University Press. Emily Jane Brontë is perhaps overshadowed by her sister Charlotte, who with Maria, Elizabeth, Branwell, and Anne made up the Brontâ family. Their father at the time of their birth was the perpetual curate of Thornhill, an imperious, eccentric man who, for instance, fed his children on potatoes without meat to make them hardy, and burnt their boots when he thought them too smart. Emily has been regarded by some as the ablest of the family, and certainly her *Wuthering Heights* and *Last Lines* are touched with genius.

229. In the *St Andrews Alumnus Chronicle 1979*. From a sermon preached by Lord Ballantrae, Chancellor of St Andrews University, to students in the university chapel. Bernard Fergusson, soldier and author, came from an old Ayrshire family, the Fergussons of Kilkerran. His distinguished military career (he was commissioned into the Black Watch, the Royal Highland Regiment, eventually becoming its Colonel) reached its peak when he served with Orde Wingate and the Chindits in Burma in the Second World War. After the war and further military operations in Palestine, Germany, and the Suez venture, Brigadier Fergusson began a new life of public service. Among the many other positions he held, he was Governor-General of New Zealand, Lord High Commissioner to the General Assembly of the Church of Scotland, and Chancellor of St Andrews University.

230. *God of a Hundred Names* Barbara Greene and Victor Gollancz, Victor Gollancz 1962 p. 205. This Latin prayer, translated by Barbara Greene, is thought to have been written by Queen Mary shortly before her execution. The fateful, tragic story of Mary has been told many times, illuminatingly so by the present Duke of Hamilton who ends his study of her life with the words: 'At eight o'clock in the morning of 8 February 1587, Mary Queen of Scots, serene, dignified and devout, met her death. She had undeniably been the victim of the grossest injustice since she fled to England. Arriving in search of political asylum, she was put on trial for a crime that was committed outside England. She was allowed neither to attend nor confront her accusers. She was not found guilty and no sentence was passed against her. Nevertheless, she was detained against her will for nineteen years without a shred of legality. Finally, she was executed, ostensibly for plotting against a queen to whom she owed no allegiance, and whose kingdom she wished to leave. In fact, she died because of something beyond her control – her dynastic proximity to the English crown.' (*Maria* R The Duke of Hamilton Mainstream Publishing 1991 p. 170).

231. James Graham, Marquis of Montrose. *The Oxford Book of Scottish Verse* John MacQueen and Tom Scott, Clarendon Press 1966 p. 263 The title of this poem is *His Metrical Prayer*. See p. 147 *supra*.

232. Holy Sonnets X in *Complete Poetry and Selected Prose of John Donne* edited by John Hayward, The Nonesuch Press 1930 p. 283. See p. 99 *supra*.

233. From the conclusion of a sermon, *Wisdom and Innocence*, preached in 1834, while Newman was Vicar of St Mary's, Oxford. The words 'of this troubled life' are not in the original. John Henry Newman remained an Anglican until 1845 when he joined the Church of Rome. Before his conversion, he had been active in promoting the Anglo-Catholic view within the Church of England, contending for the doctrine of the apostolic succession and the integrity of the Prayer Book. The *Tracts for the Times*, which he began with the support of Keble and Pusey, demonstrated the compatibility of the Thirty-Nine Articles with Catholic theology. After his accession to Rome, he became a member of the Oratorians, and established the Oratory at Birmingham. He was appointed Rector of the new Catholic University in Dublin in 1854, and in 1879 was created Cardinal of St George in Velabro. His *Lead, kindly Light* and *Apologia Pro Vita Sua* are classics of their kind. The text of his poem, *The Dream of Gerontius*, was used for the libretto of Sir Edward Elgar's oratorio of the same name. Newman also wrote two religious novels.

234. *St John 14: 1–3, 27* in the *Authorised Version* of the *Holy Bible* 1611.

235. *God of a Hundred Names* Barbara Greene and Victor Gollancz, Victor Gollancz 1962 p. 53. Part of the significance of St Polycarp is that he knew St John the Evangelist and others who 'had seen the Lord'. He was converted to Christianity while still a young man by St John. He became Bishop of Smyrna in AD 96, and died a martyr's death when a very old man.

237. In *Ionica* 1858. *They told me, Heraclitus* is a translation of an epigram on Heraclitus of Halicarnassus by the Alexandrian poet Callimachus. William Johnson Cory, educated at Eton and King's College, Cambridge, was an assistant master at Eton. He changed his name from Johnson to Cory in 1872. His *Letters and Journals* provides arresting reading.

238. In *If I Were To Tell You: Poems 1980–1993* Envoi Poets Publications, Pen Ffordd, Newport, Dyfdd, Wales p. 6. Prunella Stack founded the Woman's League of Health and Beauty in 1930, and became its President in 1982. Her first husband, Lord David Douglas-Hamilton (the youngest son of the thirteenth Duke of Hamilton), was killed in action in the Second World War. She has written several books.

239. In *National Airs*. Thomas Moore, a musician as well as a poet, became the national lyrist of Ireland. He was born in Dublin, the son of a grocer and wine merchant, was educated at Trinity College, Dublin, and became a member of the Middle Temple. He was a most engaging character, welcome everywhere for his musical talent as well as his literary skills. He matched the mood of contemporary society when he published, under the title of *Poems by the Late Thomas Little*, a volume of amorous poetry, somewhat dubious in tone and with no conspicuous literary merit except their sprightliness. His *Irish Melodies* was immediately popular, and brought him an income of £55 a year. He tried his hand at writing both novels and history,

but his forte was clearly poetry and song. His biographies of his intimate friend, Byron, however, and of Sheridan were notable in their day.

240. William Shakespeare *Sonnet 30*.

241. *Poem for the Day* edited by Nicholas Albery, Sinclair-Stevenson 1997 p. 293. *Jewels in my Hand* was written when the poet, Sasha Moorsom, was first in hospital being treated for cancer. She faced her illness, as she faced her death, with grace, dignity, and resilient equanimity.

242. *Quaker Faith and Practice* 22.95 © The Yearly Meeting of the Religious Society of Friends (Quakers) in Britain, 1995 Printed by Warwick Printing Company Limited ISBN 0 85245 269 1. *They that love beyond the world* is made up from maxims from William Penn's *The Fruits of Solitude* and *More Fruits of Solitude*. See p. 19 *supra*.

243. *Collected Poems of Stephen Spender* Faber& Faber Ltd. Stephen Spender's work includes poetry, a verse play, political and literary studies, and an autobiography. Since the Second World War, in which he served in the National Fire Service, he has lived largely in America.

244. In *The Oxford Book of Victorian Verse* Chosen by Arthur Quiller-Couch, Clarendon Press 1912 p. 330. In her early adult life, George Eliot (Mary Anne Cross, *née* Evans) had somewhat narrow religious views, but they began to expand when she translated Strauss's *Life of Jesus*, and later, Feuerbach's *Essence of Christianity*. She developed an extraordinary sense of the humour and pathos of human life, and this, together with her deep conviction of the purifying effect of human trials and of her wide learning made her great novels (*Middlemarch*, *The Mill on the Floss*) penetrating and enduring. She married John Walter Cross in May 1880 but died in December of the same year.

245. W H Auden. From *Twelve Songs IX* in *Collected Poems* Faber and Faber Ltd. See p. 192 *supra*.

246. Virginia Thesiger. In *Interpreted by Love – An Anthology of Praise* collected by Elizabeth Basset, Darton, Longman, and Tod 1994 p. 164

247. It is difficult to establish the precise history of this prayer. It seems likely that Bede Jarret, an English Dominican preacher, came across William Penn's text and worked it up into its present form.

248. In *Poems of Christina Rossetti* chosen and edited by William M Rossetti, Macmillan & Co 1904 (Golden Treasury Series) p. 234. See p. 125 *supra*.

249. *The Complete Poems of Emily Jane Brontë* edited by C W Hatfield, Oxford University Press. See p. 226 *supra*.

250. A C Swinburne. Chorus from *Atalanta in Calydon*. See p. 9 *supra*.

251. In *The Oxford Book of Scottish Verse* Chosen by Tom MacQueen and Tom Scott, Clarendon Press 1966 p. 414. *Auld Lang Syne* is the universal song of common farewell. It is essentially a folk song whose origins are unknown, which has been reworked by several poets. The best known version is this one by Burns, who never claimed it as his own but, in a letter to Mrs Dunlop of Dunlop of 17 December 1788, stated that he had amended the fragment of a 'heaven-inspired poet' and had sent it to James Johnson for inclusion in the fifth volume of *The Scots Musical Museum*. See p. 146 *supra*.

252. Published by the Souvenir Press in a book designed and illustrated by Paul Saunders 1996. A postscript to the book says that 'The poem printed in this book, by an unknown author, was found in an envelope left by a soldier killed by an exploding mine near Londonderry in 1989. It was read aloud by his father on the BBC Television programme, *Bookworm* on Remembrance Sunday, 1995, evoking a huge and warm response from viewers all over the country.'

253. *Uncle Vanya* in *Plays: Anton Chekhov* translated with an Introduction by Elisaveta Fen Penguin Books 1959 p. 244. Anton Chekhov, the Russian dramatist, began his literary career while studying medicine in Moscow by writing short humorous stories for journals. He later became closely associated with the Moscow Art Theatre, for which he wrote some of his plays, notably *The Three Sisters* and *The Cherry Orchard*.

Table of Authors and Sources

The page numbers in bold type indicate poems or prose extracts; the other numbers refer to the Notes.

Index of First Lines

293